2500

Musical Form and Transformation

DAVID LEWIN

Musical Form and Transformation: 4 Analytic Essays

YALE UNIVERSITY PRESS

NEW HAVEN AND LONDON

Set in New Baskerville type by DEKR Corporation, Woburn, Massachusetts. Printed in the United States of America by Edwards Brothers, Ann Arbor, Michigan.

Musical examples prepared by Grant Covell.

Library of Congress Cataloging-in-Publication Data

Lewin, David.
Musical form and transformation : 4 analytic essays / David Lewin.
p.   cm.
Includes bibliographical references and index.
ISBN 0-300-05686-9
1. Musical analysis.   2. Musical form.
3. Music—Theory—20th century.   I. Title.
MT90.L45   1993
781.8—dc20   92-42592
                                                                  CIP
                                                                  MN

A catalogue record for this book is available from the British Library.

10 9 8 7 6 5 4 3 2 1

for Milton,
who showed me the world of music theory,
and Allen,
who showed me how to live there

CONTENTS

CONTENTS

INTRODUCTION

My previous book, *Generalized Musical Intervals and Transformations* (Lewin 1987; henceforth *GMIT*), develops structures I called "transformational networks," arguing their pertinence for music theory and analysis. But the book contains no analysis that illustrates network organization for a particular phenomenon over some complete piece. Several readers have mentioned that to me. More generally, the book does not much engage issues of large-scale form as they interrelate with transformational analytic structure.[1] The four essays that follow constitute a response, or rather a range of responses, to the above observations.

I have tried to make the essays accessible to a general reader interested in twentieth-century music, a reader who may not have read *GMIT* or even heard of it. Technical discussions of theoretical machinery have been relegated to footnotes so far as possible. Some readers may find the essays a comfortable point of departure for subsequent exploration of *GMIT*; that would please me. Still, I conceived the new book as a free-standing edifice on its own, not as an antechamber for the older structure.

The essay on "Simbolo" (no. 1 from Dallapiccola's *Quaderno musicale*

---

1. The commentary in Lewin (1987, 231–44) on Debussy's "Reflets dans l'eau" involves a substantial section of the piece, and its commentary (pp. 225–27) on Bartók's "Syncopation" covers almost the entire piece. Still, there is not much explicit discussion of formal issues in either commentary. My article on hexachord levels in Schoenberg's "Violin Phantasy" (Lewin 1967) comes closest, among my previous writings, to providing the sort of analysis under discussion.

di Annalibera) is a concise introduction to the issue of transformational form. Measures 17–36, set off by their own tempo and textures, involve a formal variation on aspects of transformational structure over mm. 1–16. The end of that variation permits a very sharp return to opening material at m. 37 by way of closing off the piece. The abruptness of the gesture at m. 37, I claim, mirrors a certain crisis we reach just before that, a crisis that can be posed and discussed by transformational vocabulary.

The essay on Stockhausen's *Klavierstück III* was written to celebrate Wallace Berry, particularly because of his interest in musical form. The most "theoretical" of the four essays, it focuses on the forms of one pentachord reasonably ubiquitous in the piece. A special group of transformations is developed, one suggested by the musical inter-relations of the pentachord forms. Using that group, the essay arranges all pentachord forms of the music into a spatial configuration that illustrates network structure, for this particular phenomenon, over the entire piece. The temporal progression of pentachord-forms through that spatial structure suggests formal assertions about the piece. The process of network formation is compared with observations by Jeanne Bamberger (1986) on how children arrange bells to play a familiar tune. An appendix discusses the analysis of the piece by Nicholas Cook (1987); Cook's commentary seems to leave little if any room for such partial and "theoretical" studies as mine.

The essay on Webern's Orchestral Piece Op. 10, No. 4 is an homage to Allen Forte. The idea is to show how effectively transformational networks, and transformational motifs more generally, can interact with the ideas and approaches of Forte's set theory. Attention focuses first upon a certain family of objects: a hexachord H with character-istic subpentachord X, the complementary hexachord h with char-acteristic subpentachord y, and partitions of the total chromatic into H and h forms. As the music progresses, these objects are transposed or inverted more or less en masse, yielding a transformational net-work that organizes pertinent events over the entire piece. H, h, X, and y are all asymmetrical sets.

Attention then shifts to symmetrical structures: partitions of the total chromatic by trichordal derivations, an all-combinatorial hexachord Q associated with those partitions, and a characteristic symmetrical subpentachord P of Q. The symmetrical structures are interrelated by the same transformational motifs as those which participated in the H-network. Different transformations can produce the same effect upon a symmetrical set, a fact that has some interesting consequences both theoretically and analytically. It is particularly telling, in this connection, that P is a subset of H as well as of Q.

A number of observations are made about salient features of Webern's Op. 10, No. 3 and Op. 10, No. 1; these show that the analysis of Op. 10, No. 4 is not barking up the wrong tree. A fair amount of the essay involves traditional set-theoretic activity of a Fortean nature. Forte's own concise set-theoretic remarks about the piece (1973, 89–91) hold up very robustly, containing many observations of central pertinence to any set-theoretic study.

The essay on Debussy's prelude "Feux d'artifice" is the least "theoretical" of the four. Unlike the other three essays (or Lewin 1967), it does not present any network that organizes one particular phenomenon over the entire piece. It does, nevertheless, engage aspects of large-scale form as they interrelate with transformational structuring. Among such formal matters are the "polytonal" ending, the double reprise of the theme, and the progressive melodic modifications in the variations that follow the first statement of the theme. A rich complex of transformational motifs is generated over the first twenty-four measures, motifs that provide characteristic gestures for the formal profiles of various later sections. The generative process culminates at the registral climax of m. 25, preparing the entrance of the theme. A characteristic pitch-class set named APEX is attained there; characteristic transformational gestures involving various forms of APEX shape much of the "middleground" in the ensuing music. One gesture is a motion from APEX to T1(APEX); syncopation in the semitone voice-leading gives rise to characteristic subordinate sets in passing. The subordinate sets themselves also enter into some "middleground" networks, governing certain passages. I have tried to combine such commentary with a less formalist reading that takes as its point of departure the quotation, in the coda, from the *Marseillaise*.

Terms like "voice-leading" and "middleground" have a Schenker-ian flavor in this context. I have used them here mainly for their metaphorical utility, not because I wish to assert something funda-mentally Schenkerian about the techniques I employ in my study. "Middleground" suggests a pattern of progressive structural connec-tions involving temporally non-contiguous events over a bounded passage of some extent. Beyond that very general and abstract notion, there is nothing Schenkerian about my "middleground" networks, so far as my structural connections involve pitch-class transpositions/ inversions, and so far as my non-contiguous events involve various forms of non-triadic pcsets. "Syncopated voice-leading from APEX to T1(APEX)" can be considered purely formally: the pitch classes of APEX move via interval 1, one or several at a time, until all have done so. Schenker would have been happy to catalogue the inter-mediate sets that result as "passing," but he would have been aghast at the idea of attributing more autonomous harmonic significance, at some higher structural level, to the APEX forms in this context. In other contexts, "voice-leading" on my sketches may be a matter of registral commonsense, given the music. Or it may follow the law of the nearest way, with more or less plausible octave transfers, in order to get from a desired registral alignment at a point of departure to a desired registral alignment at a point of arrival. There are probably stronger canons for voice-leading in the Debussy piece, and the piece probably admits a considerably more Schenkerian approach than the one(s) I have taken. No doubt my essay would be stronger had I succeeded in working out such theoretical and analytic matters with the necessary care and effort.[2] But that is not the point of the present essay; the agenda — could it be accomplished at all — would demand another essay in its own right.

2. Parks (1989) is suggestive in this respect, although he does not discuss "Feux d'artifice." His commentaries on other piano preludes, and on other of Debussy's works, engage Fortean set theory and the more recent genera (Forte 1988b) rather than transformational structuring.

Forte (1988a) offers some strong paradigms for the sort of exploration I have in mind, and some pertinent general advice. General discussion is also to be found in Baker (1986) and Straus (1987).

Even more strongly should I emphasize that my large-scale networks for the Dallapiccola, Stockhausen, and Webern pieces are not "Ur" structures. They do not generate lower-level structure in a Chomskian sense; they do not synthesize the dialectic progressions of lower-level processes in an ultimate Hegelian *Einheit*. They are only metaphorical pictures of certain things that happen over their pieces as wholes, pictures that make manifest certain characteristic (recurrent) transformational motifs.

Generalized Musical Intervals and Transformations (*GMIT*) discusses transformations in a number of musical dimensions. Certainly, there are pieces for which one could construct large-scale networks involving rhythmic transformations. It would be interesting to study the overall organizations of "registral bands" in certain pieces, using networks that involve transformations analogous to those proposed in *GMIT* (pp. 215–17) for time spans. This would follow up on a suggestion made by John Clough (1989, 229). One could also form large-scale networks involving Riemannian or post-Riemannian transformations of Klangs. Alfred Lorenz's overall picture of *Tristan* (1926, 177–79) is a notorious prototype for such endeavors; Brian Hyer's dissertation (1989) develops more sophisticated networks for a number of extended passages in the drama.

Still, the present four essays restrict their attention to transformations that involve pitch classes, or pcsets, or series of pitch classes. I wanted to avoid fatiguing the reader with too many essays of different types, and I wanted my essays to remain within a certain mainstream of current analytic/theoretical literature in the United States.

Notes on Terminology

{x, y, z} means the unordered set comprising the three things x, y, and z. x–y–z means the three-element series whose successive members are x, y, and z, in that order.

Here and there the symbols t and e are used to stand for the numbers 10 and 11.

The essays develop many *contextually defined* operations. For instance, a certain type of configuration in the Dallapiccola piece (chap. 1) articulates the total chromatic into a pentachord and a heptachord; in that context one "J-inverts" such a configuration by inverting it so as to preserve the notes of the component pentachord en masse. In the Stockhausen piece (chap. 2), we focus upon forms of a certain pentachord — a pentachord containing a chromatic tetrachord. In *that* context one "J-inverts" such a pentachord by inverting it so as to preserve the constituent chromatic tetrachord. In the Debussy piece (chap. 4), we focus upon pitch classes and collections of pitch classes. In *that* context one "J-inverts" a pitch class (or a collection of pitch classes) by inverting it about the pitch class G as center-of-inversion. In each context the symbol J lies conveniently at hand as a *significans*; the *significandum* varies over various contexts. Readers should not attempt to carry over one meaning for "J-inversion" into another context where "J-inversion" is defined differently. The usefulness of such contextually defined operations is manifest in the essays. Occasionally I interrelate different contexts, e.g., for I-inversion of *configurations* and I-inversion of *rows* in the Dallapiccola piece. On such occasions I make my intent explicit in the text.

References to specific pitches are made according to the notation suggested by the Acoustical Society of America: The pitch class is symbolized by an upper-case letter and its specific octave placement by a number following the letter. An octave number refers to pitches from a given C through the B a major seventh above it. Cello C is C2, viola C is C3, middle C is C4, and so on. Any B♯ gets the same octave number as the B just below it; thus B♯3 is enharmonically C4. Likewise, any C♭ gets the same octave number as the C just above it; thus C♭4 is enharmonically B3.

Musical Form and Transformation

CHAPTER 1

Serial Transformation
Networks in
Dallapiccola's "Simbolo"

Example 1.1 provides the score of Dallapiccola's "Simbolo." Example 1.2 gives referential "configurations" for the pitches of the music. The configuration of mm. 1–5 comprises the "odd-dyad-out" A♯–B, shown with solid noteheads, followed by a homophonic idea shown with open noteheads. The homophony comprises three lines or voices. One line, beamed with stems up in the upper register, comprises the tones E♭–D–F–E of a BACH motif. We shall call this the "BACH line." A second line, also with stems up, starts at E♭–D and continues chromatically in register as E♭–D–D♭–C. We shall call this the "conjunct line." A third line is beamed with stems down: G♭–A♭–G–A. We shall call this the "2e2 line," since it proceeds by (pitch-class) intervals of 2, e = eleven, and 2. All three open-notehead lines fill chromatic tetrachords.

Configurations like that of mm. 1–5, as displayed in example 1.2, can clearly be transposed, inverted, and retrograded into other related configurations. Example 1.2 shows this happening in the pitch structure of the music through m. 16.

1

Example 1.1. Luigi Dallapiccola, *Quaderno musicale di Annalibera:* "Simbolo."
By kind permission of Edizioni Suvini Zerboni, Milan.

2 min. 45 secondi

The symbol "RT1" appears on example 1.2, labeling an arrow from the configuration of mm. 1–5 to the configuration of m. 6. The latter configuration is the T1-retrograde of the former. The semitone transposition here affects pitches in register, not just pitch classes. The T1-relation interacts cogently with semitonal aspects of the basic configuration itself. For instance, the low A♯1 that begins the configuration of m. 1 moves up, via RT1, to the low B1 that ends the configuration of m. 6; this reproduces on a large structural level the A♯–B dyad of the first configuration itself, the opening odd-dyad-out. The upward-beamed lines of the homophony in the first configuration end in parallel major thirds that descend a semitone: F3 descends to E3 in the BACH line; D♭3 descends to C3 in the conjunct line. Then F3 and D♭3 reappear, beginning the second configuration (at m. 6) in T1-relation to E3 and C3. A♯2 (B♭2) begins the bass of m. 6 under F3 and D♭3; that A♯2 associates with the A♯1 that underlies all of mm. 1–5 as part of the ostinato pedal. In particular, A♯1, D♭3, and F3 sound together on the downbeat of M. 4; A♯ there is the lowest note of the piece so far and F the highest. The B♭- (A♯-) minor triad then returns in m. 6, supporting the {F,D♭} connection.

The second verticality of the m. 6 configuration is an order-segment of the "original row," but since we have not heard any well-ordered row in the music yet, there is not much to make of that. We have no way of "knowing," as yet, that G♭–A♭–D in mm. 2–3 forms an order-segment in some row pertinent to the music. So we will not (yet) hear the "trichord {G♭,A♭,D}" of mm. 2–3 as specially marked in T11-relation to the trichord {G,D♭,F} of m. 4; nor will we hear {G♭,A♭,D} "returning," in that connection, at m. 6, where our attention is rather on the fresh high note F♯4. Only later (mm. 18–19) does a trichord-relationship in a new configuration suggest a segmental trichord-relationship within some possible row.

Because of the T1-relation between the m. 1 and the m. 6 configurations, the total span of each polyphonic voice expands, from the chromatic tetrachord over mm. 1–5 to a chromatic pentachord over mm. 1–6. Thus the BACH voice, which spanned {D,E♭,E,F} over mm. 1–5, expands to cover {D,E♭,E,F,F♯} over mm. 1–6. Likewise,

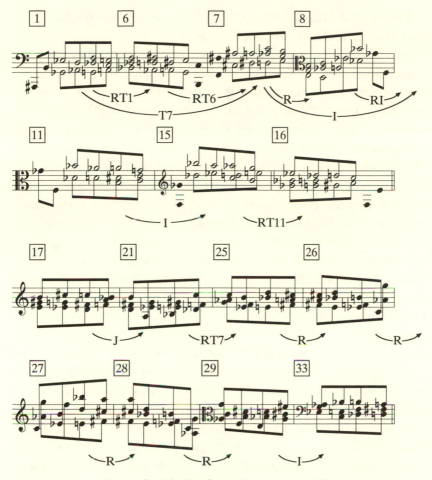

Example 1.2. Configurations, mm. 1 –37.

the conjunct voice expands from the range {C,D♭,D,E♭} over mm. 1–5 to the range {C,D♭,D,E♭,E} over mm. 1–6. And the 2e2 voice expands similarly, from {G♭,G,A♭,A} to {G♭,G,A♭,A,B♭}. The chromatic pentachord will assume greater autonomy later on, as we shall see.

From m. 6 to m. 7, as example 1.2 shows with its "RT6" arrow, the configuration shifts by retrograde tritone-transposition. As before, the transformation applies to pitches in register, not just to pitch classes. The BACH voice in m. 7 at last presents the motive at the "correct" pitch-class level (A#–A–C–B).[1]

The RT6 transformation interacts very cogently with configuration-structuring. The melodically climactic incipit dyad F–F# of the m. 6 configuration becomes the opening odd-dyad-out {F,F#} of the m. 7 configuration, while the final odd-dyad-out {C,B} of the m. 6 configuration becomes the melodically climactic cadence dyad C–B of the m. 7 configuration. (In each case, the melodic climax involves the highest pitches heard so far in the piece.) The 2e2 voice of the m. 6 polyphony, Bb–Ab–A–G, spans the same chromatic tetrachord as does the conjunct voice in m. 7, Bb–A–Ab–G. Likewise the conjunct voice of m. 6, Db–D–D#–E, spans the same tetrachord as does the 2e2 voice of m. 7, C#–D#–D–E.

The A#-minor triad appears in the texture of m. 7, embedded "in second inversion." The T7 relation between mm. 1–5 and m. 7 is aurally marked via the Eb-minor triad of m. 2 plus the Bb-minor triads of m. 6 and m. 7.

In that connection, one notes that the registral transfer an octave up, during the configuration of m. 8, is carried out exactly by the pitch classes Eb (in the 2e2 voice) and Bb (in the other two polyphonic voices); when all three polyphonic voices have moved up an octave, the odd-dyad-out naturally moves up as well. The registral transfer is carried out while the configuration of m. 8 is retrograding that of m. 7.

Over mm. 9–10, as the odd-dyad-out of the m. 8 configuration begins to "walk" in the manner of m. 1, we begin to recognize more directly the [R]T7 relation between the configurations of m. 1 and m. 8. We recognize, that is, a "fifth-relation" between the walking dyad A#–B of mm. 1–5 and the walking dyad F–Gb of mm. 8–9. At m. 11, then, we may well believe that we are about to hear "the opening of the piece repeated on the dominant." That is, we anticipate hearing at m. 11 the texture of mm. 1–5 applied to the pitch

1. It may puzzle some readers that the BACH line does not appear at the "correct" level in mm. 1–6. I believe that the music of mm. 1–2 (–3) is intended to refer to the opening of Liszt's BACH Fantasy.

configuration of m. 7 (played an octave higher), a configuration T7-related to the configuration of mm. 1–5. The B♭-minor triad embedded in m. 11 whets that anticipation all the more.

But, instead of the m. 7 configuration, we get that configuration inverted about its odd-dyad-out. An arrow labeled RI extends, on example 1.2, from the configuration of m. 8 to that of m. 11. The m. 11 configuration is thus in I-relation to the m. 7 configuration. Besides preserving the odd-dyad-out from the m. 7 configuration to that of m. 11, the I-relationship maps the tetrachordal span of the 2e2 voice, m. 7 configuration, into the span of the conjunct voice, m. 11 configuration. Specifically, C♯–D♯–D–E is the 2e2 voice of the m. 7 configuration; D♭–D–E♭–E, with the same span, is the conjunct voice of the m. 11 configuration. Similarly, the conjunct voice of the m. 7 configuration, A♯–A–A♭–G, covers the same tetrachordal span as does the 2e2 voice B♭–A♭–A–G of the m. 11 configuration. We have already observed that the tetrachordal spans for the conjunct and 2e2 voices are invariant in moving from the configuration of m. 6 to that of m. 7. So those (pitch-class) spans remain invariant from m. 6 to m. 15 on example 1.2. Actually, they remain invariant through m. 15, since the configuration of m. 15 is that of m. 11 an octave higher, so far as the 2e2 and conjunct voices are concerned.

The operation I, it will be noted, was not defined as "inversion about F and F♯," or as "inversion about C, followed by T11." It was not defined with reference to any pitch classes whatsoever. Rather, it was defined with respect to a "contextual" feature of the configuration(s) upon which it operates. To apply I to a given configuration, invert that configuration about its odd-dyad-out. This sort of "inversion" operation differs from those defined by pitch-class centers. We shall have occasion to use other such "contextual" inversion operations later in this book.[2]

The configuration of m. 15 applies the operation I to the configuration of m. 11. This restores the configuration of m. 7, so far as pitch classes are concerned. Indeed, the pitches of the homophony

2. Michael Cherlin (1983) discusses contextual inversion operations, using them most effectively for analyzing Leitmotiv-like partitionings in *Moses und Aron*.

are the same, two octaves higher, except that the "C" and the "H" of the BACH voice are an octave "too low" in m. 15. As always since m. 8, B♭ is (therefore) the highest note of the configuration. Measure 15 provides the "return of mm. 1–5 on the dominant" that we anticipated earlier, except that the rhythm is now so changed (and the register so far away) that the "return" has little force here, as compared to m. 11 with its moving bass. Each pitch in the homophony of m. 15 lies exactly an octave above the corresponding pitch of mm. 11–14.

The configuration of m. 16 is in RT11 relation to that of m. 15. RT11 here "undoes" the effect of RT1 earlier, and aspects of the m. 1 configuration reemerge. The m. 16 configuration is in RT6 relation to the m. 1 configuration. The tetrachordal span of the conjunct voice E♭–D–D♭–C, in the m. 1 configuration, reemerges as the span of the 2e2 voice E♭–D♭–D–C, in the m. 16 configuration. And the tetrachordal span of the 2e2 voice G♭–A♭–G–A, in the m. 1 configuration, reemerges as the span of the conjunct voice G♭–G–G♯–A, in the m. 16 configuration. We also hear an E♭-minor triad leading off the polyphony of the m. 16 configuration, and we associate that with the E♭-minor triad embedded in the music of m. 2. The two E♭-minor triads associate across all the intervening B♭-minor triads mm. 6, 7, 9, 11, 15). The tetrachordal spans of the conjunct and the 2e2 voices associate between the m. 1 configuration of example 2 and the m. 16 configuration; among all the intervening configurations (mm. 6, 7, 8, 11, 15) the spans of the same voice also associate.

The upper (2e2) voice of the m. 16 configuration picks up (in the same register) the notes D♭–E♭–{C,D} from the lower part of the right hand at the beginning of m. 15. The right-hand G♭ of m. 16 merges with the left-hand G♭ in the music; accordingly a "lower line" B♭–G–G♯–A emerges in the right hand there. Its tetrachordal span reproduces, an octave lower, the span of the conjunct line from the right hand in m. 15, B♭–A–A♭–G. As these observations show, the integrity of the original polyphonic voices, as chromatic-tetrachord generators, is becoming compromised. Over mm. 17–20 a new configuration will emerge, governing a new large section of the piece.

Example 1.3 graphs in a compact network the serial transforma-

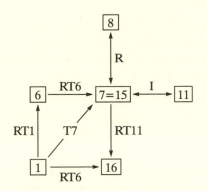

Example 1.3. Network of serial transformations interrelating the configurations of mm. 1–16.

tions of the piece discussed so far. The numbers inside the boxed nodes stand for the corresponding configurations on example 1.2. "7 = 15" indicates that the pitch-class configuration of m. 15 on example 1.2 is the same as the pitch class configuration of m. 7 on that example. On example 1.3, "RT1" and "RT11" operations label vertical arrows (upward and downward) between the bottom row and the middle row. "RT6" labels horizontal arrows between the left column and the middle column. "R" labels a vertical arrow between the top row and the middle row; "I" labels a horizontal arrow between the middle column and the right column. Between the configuration of m. 1 and the configuration of m. 7, "T7" labels a diagonal arrow pointing up and to the right.

At m. 17 the musical texture changes, as does the type of configuration; the tempo increases as well.[3] The new configuration of m. 17, as shown on example 1.2, partitions the total chromatic into

3. The tempo increase is by a factor somewhere between 11/10 and 8/7. 84 × (11/10) = 92.4; 84 × (8/7) = 96. 10/9 seems the easiest ratio to practice. Using this ratio, the five eighth notes of m. 17 are equal in duration to the four eighth notes of m. 1 plus an extra sixteenth (in the old tempo). One can pick up that duration from the last four eighths of m. 16 plus the dot of the dotted eighth that precedes them. N.B.: there is no ritard in m. 16.

a chromatic pentachord (beamed solid noteheads, stems up) and a chromatic heptachord (beamed solid noteheads, stems down.[4] The pentachord comprises the "correct" notes of BACH plus C♯.

The new configuration for mm. 17–20, on example 1.2, can be compared with example 1.4, which shows the way in which the old configuration-type would analyze this music. The heptachord of the new configuration comprises the BACH voice of the old configuration, plus its conjunct voice, plus the note D4. D4 provides another stepwise semitone E♭–D in the voice-leading; it also provides another major third (D–F♯) to accompany the BACH voice. The old 2e2 voice, on example 1.4, is broken up; the B–C♯–C that remains from it is combined with the odd-dyad-out {A,B♭} to form the new chromatic pentachord of example 1.2, mm. 17–20.

Another form of the new configuration appears on example 1.2 at m. 21. The m. 21 configuration is the m. 17 configuration subjected to "J-inversion." To J-invert the new type of configuration, one inverts it so as to preserve its constituent pentachord and also its constituent heptachord. Thus J inverts the configuration of m. 17 so as to preserve the total content {A,B♭,B,C,C♯} of the constituent pentachord and also the total content of the constituent heptachord. Moreover, J here preserves the individual vertical dyads {E,G♯}, {E♭,G}, and {D,F♯} within the heptachord while retrograding their order of appearance in the configuration of m. 21. The entire heptachord is

Example 1.4. Hypothetical analysis of mm. 17–20 in the old configuration mode.

4. The partitioning is somewhat forced as compared to the more obvious partition into four consecutive trichords. The point of the asserted partition is to maintain and develop the idea of unidirectional chromatic sliding, with some organal major thirds (heptachord), counterpointed by some non-unidirectional line that spans a chromatic cluster (pentachord). The heptachord lies at G♯ or below, the pentachord at A or above.

preserved in register. The B and C of the pentachord are preserved as B4 and C5; A and B♭ transfer down an octave in the m. 21 configuration, followed by C♯/D♭. As example 1.4 shows, {A,B♭} would be the odd-dyad-out in the old configuration for mm. 17–20. B♭ and A have been the highest notes of the piece so far, as B♭5–A5 in m. 15. The pitch class B♭ has been characteristically mobile in register throughout the music so far. A♯1, in m. 1, is the first and lowest note of the piece. B♭4, in m. 9, is the highest note of the piece so far, displaced in register to become so, as shown in the m. 8 configuration of example 1.2. B♭4 remains as highest note in the m. 11 configuration; then B♭5 becomes the highest note of m. 15 and of the music to that point. Thus the octave displacement of B♭, from the m. 17 configuration to the m. 21 configuration, is thematic.

At the m. 25 configuration, A and B♭ (and C♯) return to the register of the m. 17 configuration. The dyad {G4,G♯,4} — the highest dyad of the component heptachord in the m. 17 configuration and again in the m. 21 configuration — becomes the odd-dyad-out for the m. 25 configuration. In that configuration the correct BACH tetrachord is displayed in the conjunct line C–B–B♭–A. The tessitura of the m. 25 configuration is exactly one semitone above that of the m. 17 configuration; this recalls the registral semitone rise from the configuration of m. 1 to the configuration of m. 6. No serial T1 is involved, however, between the configurations of m. 17 and m. 25. Rather, m. 25 is RT7 of m. 21 (and hence RT7J of m. 17), so far as configurations are concerned. The T7 aspect of the relationship is most easily heard between the last verticality of the m. 21 configuration and the first verticality of the m. 25 configuration — also between the opening B-minor triad of m. 21 and the closing F♯-minor triad of m. 25.

Once stated, the pitch-class configuration of m. 25 remains in effect, alternating with its retrograde, through the configurations of m. 26, m. 27, m. 28, and m. 29 on example 1.2. The musical textures change and a number of registral transfers are given rein. In m. 26, C moves down an octave and G up an octave. In m. 27, F, B♭, and A move up an octave; the climax on B♭5–A5 audibly recalls the earlier mobility on B♭ that culminated at m. 15 on B♭5–A5. B♭5 remains the highest note of the piece. At m. 28, B♭ and F move back down, as does G. The A remains high. The C of m. 29 remains low, sounding together with the low G. A♭ also becomes low, moving down an octave to sound under the low {C,G} in the last verticality of the configuration.

That positioning of the {A♭,C,G} trichord is the point of departure for the configuration of mm. 29–32, which repositions its pitches so that they lie exactly 5 semitones in register below the analogous pitches in the configuration of mm. 21–24. Thus an RT7-relation is quite audible between those two configurations (mm. 21–24 and mm. 29–32), even though RT7 is not so immediately audible between mm. 21–24 and the temporally contiguous m. 25. In the configuration of mm. 29–32, the conjunct voice spans its chromatic tetrachord at the BACH level, as C–B–B♭–A; this leads directly on to the oscillating G–A♭ dyad of m. 33 in the music.

{G,A♭} is the "odd-dyad-out" for the configuration of mm. 33–35, which I-inverts the configuration of mm. 29–32 about that dyad. We have noted special things about the placement of the dyad in m. 29 of the music, and again at m. 33 of the music, after which its oscillation persists for two more measures (34–35). Indeed, we also noted {G,G♯} at the top of the component heptachord at mm. 17–20 and again at mm. 21–24. It is not quite accurate to refer to the dyad as an "odd-dyad-out" in the configurations of m. 25, m. 29, and m. 33. The new configurations, from m. 17 onward, do not contain "odd-dyads-out." Hence the operation I, "inversion about the odd-dyad-out," is not defined on those configurations, strictly speaking. To speak strictly of "applying I," both to the configuration of m. 7 and to the configuration of m. 29, we shall have to invoke some stronger ordering from which both types of configurations can be derived, and then imagine the operation I being applied to that stronger ordering in both cases, noting the effect of already-applied-I on each type of configuration. In short, we shall need something like the row B♭–B–E♭–G♭–A♭–D–D♭–F–G–C–A–E, which can be asserted as "the row of the work" when one analyzes the *Quaderno* as a whole.

Any form of this row will have a semitone dyad either as its first two notes or as its last two notes. We can then define the operation I *on a given form of the row* as inversion-about-the-notes-of-the-bound-

ary-semitone. So, for instance, I(F–F♯–A♯–C♯– . . .) = G♭–F–D♭–B♭–
. . . The row F–F♯–A♯–C♯– . . . controls the configuration of m. 7,
and the row G♭–F–D♭–B♭– . . . controls the configuration of m. 11;
the two configurations are "I-inversions" in this new sense. The fact
that they share odd-dyads-out now follows from the already defined
I-row relationship; it is not a defining aspect of an I-configuration
relationship. The same holds for I(G–A♭–C–D♯– . . .) = A♭–G–E♭–
C– . . . And those two row forms control the configurations of mm. 29
and 33 on example 1.2. The fact that the two configurations share
{G,A♭} dyads in their opening verticalities falls out from the already
defined I-row relationship; it is not a defining aspect of an I-configuration relationship.

That said, we can note that both the m. 29 and m. 33 configurations
have {G,A♭} as the non-BACH-voice dyad in their opening verticalities, and that both configurations have {F♯,A} as the non-BACH-voice
dyad in their final verticalities. In the textures presented in the music,
the {G,A♭}s and {F♯,A}s all oscillate to and fro while the notes of the
BACH voices sustain like a cantus firmus.

The left side of example 1.5 reproduces example 1.3; the right
side adds a transformational summary for the configurations after
m. 17 as discussed above. One sees from the visual motifs of the
example how clearly the transformational picture of mm. 21–36 can
be regarded as a variation on a substructure from the picture of

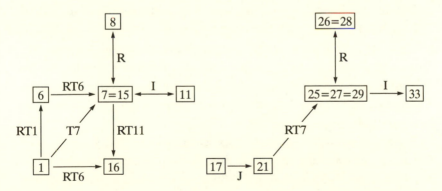

Example 1.5. The transformational picture of mm. 21–36 varies a substructure from the picture of mm. 1–16.

mm. 1–16. The RT7 arrow from "21" to "25 = 27 = 29" corresponds to the T7 arrow from "1" to "7 = 15." The R arrow that connects "25 = 27 = 29" and "26 = 28" corresponds to the R arrow that connects "7 = 15" and "8." The I arrow that connects "25 = 27 = 29" and "33" corresponds to the I arrow that connects "7 = 15" and "11."

The common gestural profile that links the left and right parts of example 1.5 as "variations" can be described as follows. After some preliminary maneuvering, an early configuration is transposed by T7 (and possibly retrograded). The result is then elaborated by its retrograde; it is also elaborated by its I-inversion.

The profile emerges strongly from example 1.5. It would be hard to render it so clear or precise without the transformational apparatus at hand. Not only is the idea suggestive in itself; it also gives an interesting rationale for the return of the (retrograde) opening configuration at m. 37, as we shall soon see.

First, we can observe that the characteristic walking dyad on A♯1–B2, which suddenly returns in m. 37, "should" come at the end of the retrograded configuration-form, not at its beginning. Its premature return in m. 37 makes the formal articulation there very sharp for the listener. Without such articulation, we would pay a lot more attention to links like {C3,E3}–{D♭3,F3}, a dyad-pair in the heptachordal polyphony of mm. 34–35 and also in the BACH-plus-conjunct polyphony of m. 38. We discussed that dyad-pair earlier, as it relates to the upper register of mm. 4–5 and to the connection of {C3,E3} to {D♭3,F3} at the beginning of m. 6.

Example 1.5 shows why m. 37, after the configuration of mm. 33–36, is a plausible place for a big formal articulation. By m. 37 the "variation" portrayed by the right side of the example has essentially finished its work, once the I-arrow has linked "29" to "33." Something new can now happen.

Even more telling is a psychological rationale that suggests why something new should happen at this moment. To assert an I-relation between mm. 29–32 and mm. 33–36, as in our earlier discussion, has entailed our obtruding the idea of rows into a piece based so far on configurations. This precipitates a critical point in our reception of the music. We may not be fully aware of the crisis, to be sure, but perhaps we sense it obscurely, as suggested by the composer's indication *oscuro* on the critical {G,A♭} dyad at m. 33. Given this state of affairs, something large should happen in the form just after mm. 33–36. Perhaps a row will appear in the music. Perhaps some new configuration-type will appear — possibly generating a new "variation." Or perhaps the piece will close, as it in fact does, via the references to the original configuration in mm. 37–42 and then in mm. 42–46. The enigmatic effect of those references is not simply due to a *Stimmung* inherent in the material itself. Rather, our puzzlement involves a sense of incompleteness; the music withdraws from us, withholding something from us — that is, the row. We are impelled onwards to the following pieces of the *Quaderno*.

I have not asserted any transformational relation that generates the configuration of mm. 17–20 from any earlier configuration. That is because the change of configuration-type, together with other changes in texture and tempo, emphasizes mm. 17–20 as a new beginning to my ear. In addition, it works well on the picture of example 1.5 not to have an arrow leading into "17" from the left; this emphasizes the variation structure.

One could try to assert various transformational relations between earlier material and the configuration of example 1.4. For instance, example 1.4 inverts the configuration of mm. 1–5 about B♭. We have noted on several occasions the role of B♭ over the piece in defining registral extremes and registral shifts. But inverting about a pitch class is something we have avoided so far. More consistent with our procedure would be to regard example 1.4 as T5 of the I-inversion of the m. 16 configuration. That analysis, however, seems to posit an imaginary configuration interpolated between the m. 16 configuration and example 1.4. And that seems dubious. When all is said and done, I remain most comfortable leaving "17" on example 1.5 without any arrow pointing toward it.

CHAPTER 2

Making and Using a
Pcset Network for
Stockhausen's *Klavierstück III*

In this chapter I propose to develop a transformational network analysis that will organize and interrelate all (0,1,2,3,6) pentachords over Stockhausen's *Klavierstück III* (1952). Since the analysis is intended partly as a methodological model, I shall be quite self-conscious about my methodology in a number of respects. I shall discuss why I assert pentachord-forms that Jonathan Harvey does not (1975, 26), and why I do not assert some forms that he does.[1] I shall discuss why, in constructing my network, I use the particular transformations that I do; some of these transformations operate upon complete forms of the pentachord (0,1,2,3,6) but not upon other pitch-class sets, nor upon individual pitch classes.

Finally, and most important, I shall discuss certain issues involved in choosing to assert this or that abstract network as analytically

---

1. Although I diverge from Harvey (1975) on technical matters here (and elsewhere), I admire strongly the success of the book as a whole. It gives a very clear and true picture of its subject.

pertinent. Rather than asserting a network that follows pentachord relations one at a time, according to the chronology of the piece, I shall assert instead a network that displays all the pentachord forms used and all their potentially functional interrelationships, in a very compactly organized little spatial configuration. This network cannot depict for us how the piece moves through chronological time. But that is not necessarily a methodological disadvantage, for we can view the chronological progress of the piece as a path, or a series of path-segments, through the network. And that is interesting, both theoretically and analytically.[2] The piece, in this sense, makes several "passes" through sections of its network; the beginnings and endings of the path-segments thereby acquire special functions. Furthermore, as the path-segments fill or suggest the totality of the network, they constitute one way in which the piece, articulated chronologically into its several "passes," projects form.

The final section of this chapter will view these matters in connection with some recent work in musical cognition (Bamberger 1986). This cognitive study observes the various ways in which children attempt to configure a family of bells, not only in order to model the structure of a tune in a compact spatial arrangement, but also to facilitate its performance through ordered gestural paths.

Example 2.1 reproduces the score of the Stockhausen piece. Example 2.2 abstracts the successive pitch classes of the music into integer notation, with "t" for 10 and "e" for 11; this succession is presented in the example via the string of symbols 9e28t . . . (that is, A,B,D,A♭,B♭ . . .) that runs near the top. The bar lines of the score are reproduced on example 2.2 as vertical dividers along the string of symbols, and a measure number is given in the example at the top of every fifth measure. When two pitches are attacked simultaneously in the music, even if they are released at different times, I count the pitch classes as "simultaneous" for present purposes; example 2.2 indicates the simultaneity by including the pitch classes involved

---

2. Lewin (1987) touches on certain related matters but not in connection with any complete composition. The material in Lewin (1987), sections 9.6 and 9.7, is relevant to some extent.

III

U. E. 12251 LW

Example 2.1. Stockhausen NR. 2 KLAVIERSTUECKE III only. © Copyright 1954 by Universal Edition (London) Ltd., London. © Copyright renewed. All rights reserved. Used by permission of European American Music Distributors Corporation, sole U.S. and Canadian agent for Universal Edition (London).

within parentheses. So, for example, m. 3 of the symbol-string on the example contains the notation "(87)"; this symbolizes pitch classes for the A♭ and the G that are attacked simultaneously in m. 3 of the music.

Below the running string of symbols on example 2.2, various forms of the pentachord are extracted and displayed. The first such form

5

9e28t9 | 8e5324 | (87) | 6 | 54t | 2(3e) | (859) | (1t)45 | cont.

```
P:    9e28t9 | 8e              t | 2( e) | (8 9) | ( t)
p:       8t9 | 8e5             t |  ( e) | (859) | ( t)
p6:         e5324           4 | 2(3e) | ( 5 )
P6:         5324 | (8  )    4 | 2(3 ) | (85 )
p9:            2 | (87) | 6 | 5
P8:               4 | ( 7) | 6 | 54t
```

10   15

cont. | (1t)45 | 637 | 4(e8t)0 | 9(714)853 | 6e43 | 2(1t) | 8 | 709 | e

```
P8:          45 | 6 7 | 4( t)
p8:      (1 )45 | 6 7 | 4        ; (714) 5 | 6
P9:           5 | 6 7 | (e8 ) ; (7  )85 | 6e
P1:           3 | (e t)0 | 9
P2:              (e t)0 | ( 14)
p6:                             53 | e43 | 2
p5:                             43 | 2(1t)
Pe:                             (1t) | 8 | 7 9
p2:                             (1t) |  | 70 | e
```

Example 2.2. Successive pitch classes of the piece in integer notation; various forms of the P/p pentachord.

to appear is labeled P (for pentachord); the next such form is labeled p (lower-case); it is an inverted form of P. The form p6 is the 6-transpose of p; the form P6 is the 6-transpose of P, and so forth. A certain analytic bias is built into this notation: we are asserting a notational priority for the forms labeled P and p; we are also privileging notationally the particular inversional relationship between them, and more generally between forms labeled Pn and pn. These notational biases will not constrain our imagination so long as we remain conscious of our methodology and are prepared to shift the notation as later analytical work may suggest.

Having decided to undertake the present exercise, I reviewed Harvey's analysis (1975); then, putting it aside, I went through the score myself, hunting for pentachord forms by ear. The resulting catalogue of forms referenced every pitch class in the piece except for pitch class 3 in m. 9 and pitch class e in m. 16. Intellectually, I decided that I should assert pentachord forms to embed those pitch classes. I found and asserted the P1 form of mm. 9–11 and the p2 form of mm. 13–16; these seemed the most plausible candidates for the job. Next I checked my work up to this point against Harvey's analysis, prepared to add more forms to my list if I decided that they fit well with what I had already asserted. The only such form I recall finding was the P8 form of mm. 8–10.[3]

I now had the catalogue of forms displayed on example 2.2. The forms I list that Harvey does not are these: p6 in m. 2, p9 in mm. 2–5, p6 and P6 in mm. 5–7, P in mm. 5–8, p8 in mm. 8–10, p6 in mm. 11–13, Pe in mm. 13–15. Those forms which Harvey lists that I do not are shown on example 2.3. The pcset labeled "??" is not a form of P; I conjecture that Harvey meant to cite the form labeled "intending P7 again?"

Having reached this point (but not before!), I discovered the logic by which I had included the forms of example 2.2 and excluded those of example 2.3. Essentially, the forms I assert are projected in "tightly packed" order-spans of the running pitch-class string; the forms also

```
        5                        10                          15
        |54t|2(3e)|(859)|(1t)45|637|4(e8t)0|9(714)853|6e43|2(1t)|8|709|e

p5:      4 |2(3 )|(   )|(1t)
P7:                         5|63 |4(   ) |9
??:                                    53|6 4 | (  )|  |7   ??
intending P7 again?                 9(   ) 53|6 4
Pt:                                     6   | (  )|8|709
```

Example 2.3. Pentachord forms asserted by Harvey (1975) but not displayed in example 2.2.

3. Some readers may be growing impatient with this "unscientific" narrative. Do not worry; you will presently have "science" galore. The narrative reflects my conviction that one cannot be methodologically thorough in reporting an intellectual exercise without reporting the conditions under which the exercise was carried out.

reference every pitch-class event of the piece. Those notions can be made precise as follows. We define a form-citation on example 2.2 or example 2.3 to be "of deficiency n" if its temporal span jumps over exactly n order-positions in the running string of pitch classes. So, on example 2.2, the first four citations (of P, p, p6, and P6 during mm. 1–3) are all of deficiency 0; none of these citations hops over any order-position in the running string. The citation of p9 in mm. 2–5 is of deficiency 1; it omits reference to the last order-position of m. 2. The citation of P8 in mm. 2–5 is of deficiency 0. It is not of deficiency 1; though the citation fails to reference pc 8 in m. 3, it still references the one and only *order*-position in m. 3, the order-position represented by the begin-to-end parentheses. Similarly, the citation of P in mm. 5–8 is of deficiency 0 (and not deficiency 3); the concomitant citation of p is of deficiency 1 (since it hops over the first order-position of m. 6).

Continuing in this fashion, we can see the logic of example 2.2. It cites every form of deficiency 0 and every form of deficiency 1 that can be extracted from the running string. Example 2.2 also cites three forms of deficiency 2, namely P1 in mm. 9–11, p8 in mm. 11–12, and p2 in mm. 13–16. P1 and p2 can be justified as suggested earlier; they are needed to reference the respective pitch classes 3 in m. 9 and e in m. 16; they are the forms of least possible deficiency that reference those pitch classes. The p8 form of mm. 11–12 runs concomitantly with a P9 form (of deficiency 1); this makes sense as a recollection of the concomitant p8 and P9 heard shortly before, over mm. 8–10. Furthermore, the p8-and-P9 relation seems intellectually suggestive in connection with the p9-and-P8 relation of mm. 2–5. The earlier relation stands out on example 2.2 because the other forms cited over mm. 1–8 seem to be elaborating a sort of P-p-P6-p6 grouping.

Such ideas are already beginning to suggest aspects of an eventual network-model. Before proceeding to construct that model, however, I should note that my excluding the forms of example 2.3 is consistent with the logic just developed. The p5 form of example 2.3 is of deficiency 2; the two P7 forms are of deficiency 3, and the Pt form is of deficiency 5. I might be persuaded through repeated listening to admit on my list the p5 form and the two P7 forms, but I find the Pt form of deficiency 5 too remote to accept either intellectually or by ear.[4]

Let us now start constructing a network to assert various sorts of organization and interrelation among the forms of example 2.2. A good way to begin is by informally looking over the example for signs of any organization or interrelation that one might want to use in the network. We have already noticed a few such signs. The first four forms on the example, P, p, p6, and P6 over mm. 1–3, form a grouping that returns en masse over mm. 5–8. We shall want to assert the grouping in our network and to devote special attention to inter-relationships we might want to assert involving pairs of forms from among the four. It will be convenient to give the grouping a name; let us call it the "0/6 complex."

Against the opening exposition of that complex and its return in mm. 5–8, the isolated pair of forms p9 and P8 stands out in strong contrast during mm. 2–5. The form P8 returns in mm. 8–10 as almost the first form asserted after the second exposition of the 0/6 complex. Over mm. 8–10, P8 is concomitant with both p8 and P9. A number of relationships are suggested.

First, P8 and p8 concomitantly suggest that the initial 0/6 complex may be subject to transposition: P8-and-p8 is the 8-transpose of P-and-p; it is also the 2-transpose of P6-and-p6. Is this a constructive relation in the piece? That is not yet clear, but we can tuck the

---

4. I hope it is clear that I do not propose the "logic" of my decision algorithm here as a general rule for the analysis of set structure in pertinent music. For example, in cataloguing significant forms for the basic pentachord of Schoenberg's *Klavierstück* Op. 23, No. 3, a different logic obtains: Thematic contour, dynamics, attack characters, register, and relative register all articulate in that piece polyphonic textures — explicit and implicit — that can project significant pentachord forms of relatively high deficiency. So far I have not been able to hear, or even see, this sort of structuring at work in Stockhausen's piece. The "logic" of the catalogue within example 2.2 does not reflect the application of some universal rule; rather it reflects a certain consistency in my hearing and thinking about that particular piece, or rather in my *having heard* and thought about it. The logic is useful for checking the consistency and completeness of the hearing, which should certainly not be arbitrary or sporadic.

question away, noting that P2 is asserted in mm. 10–11 — very shortly after P8-and-p8 — and that the last cited form on example 2.2 is p2.

Returning to mm. 8–10, we can speculate on p8-and-P9 there: Does their relation have something to do with the earlier presentation of p9-and-P8 in mm. 2–5? The notation is suggestive, but we must be careful not to attribute too much significance to the notation, which comes with the built-in bias discussed earlier. If we look at the sets involved, we find that p9-to-P8, as over mm. 2–5, preserves the tri-chord {5,6,7} and replaces the tritone {2,8} by the tritone {4,t}. In comparison, p8-to-P9, as over mm. 8–10, preserves the trichord {5,6,7} and replaces the minor third {1,4} by the minor third {8,e}. It is not immediately clear that we will want to assert a functional relation between p9-to-P8 (mm. 2–5) and p8-to-P9 (mm. 8–10). On the other hand, the notation does reflect a possible, more indirect sort of relation that we can always assert if we want to. Since p8 and P9 return concomitantly over mm. 11–12, there does seem to be some compositional stress on the idea. But, as discussed earlier, the p8 of mm. 11–12 is of deficiency 2, and it is not needed to embed any particular pitch class of the piece.

Leaving the matter there for the time being, let us focus now on a possible significant relation involving the concomitant P8 and P9 over mm. 8–10. The most obvious relation to consider is P9 = T1(P8): P9 is the 1-transpose of P8. This does seem to be a significantly recurring relationship. Right after the presentation of P8-and-P9 in mm. 8–10, the next two forms listed on example 2.2 are P1 and P2 = T1(P1). After the return of p8-and-P9 in mm. 11–12, the next new forms are p6 and p5; p6 = T1(p5). Following the chronology of the form-presentations, we can also write p5 = Te(p6); Te (transposition by 11) is the inverse operation of T1. The T1-idea thus does seem to be highly constructive over the second half of the piece.[5]

5. (P8)u(P9), the set-theoretic union of P8 and P9, is the heptachord {4,5,6,7,8,t,e}; this is the complement of the pentachord {0,1,2,3,9}, which is p4. Similarly, (P1)u(P2) is the complement of p9, while (p5)u(p6) is the complement of Pt. The forms p4, p9, and Pt are not otherwise referenced by example 2.2, however. Example 2.3 does assert Pt, but, as I said earlier, I cannot accept this form of deficiency 5 in the present context.

Pe-to-p2, the progression of the "final cadence," transposes the progression P6-to-p9, a progression that we can assert as a means of leaving the opening 0/6 complex during mm. 2–5. Notationally, this P6-to-p9 suggests considering as well a functional P9-to-p6 progression over mm. 11–13. As with the earlier idea of relating p9-to-P8 and p8-to-P9, we shall tuck this idea away for the time being.

Earlier we considered the idea of imagining a secondary "2/8 complex" to go with our 0/6 complex. Let us review that notion again. Asserting a 2/8 complex is supported by several features of example 2.2. The forms P8 and p8 are both cited twice on the example (though the second citation of p8, of deficiency 2, is perhaps a bit shaky). P8 and p8 initiate what is in some sense "the second half of the piece," that is, the events of mm. 8–16 that follow upon the last exposition of the 0/6 complex. P2 of mm. 10–11 bridges the two p8-citations of mm. 8–10 and mm. 11–12; p2 is the final form cited.

It is tempting, in any case, to take the basic relationships exposed so heavily by the 0/6 complex during mm. 1–8 as referential for later structuring too. If we adopt that point of view, we shall notice not only the possibility of asserting a 2/8 complex, but also the possibility of asserting two more complexes, both incomplete. Specifically, the p9 of mm. 2–5 and the P9s of mm. 8–10 and mm. 11–12 form part of an incomplete 3/9 complex; part of another incomplete complex is formed by the overlapping successive forms p5 and Pe of mm. 13–15.

So much for our preliminary overview of example 2.2. We should now decide just what are the "basic relationships exposed . . . by the 0/6 complex." It is certainly safe to assert that one of them is T6, the

---

In general, (Pn)u(P(n + 1)) = compl.(p(n + 8)); (p(n − 1))u(pn) = compl. (P(n + 4)). The complement relations would be highly significant for a Fortean set-theoretic analysis. I do not assert them in the present context because the network I am constructing addresses only forms of the P-pentachord; it will not address heptachords as well. I could devise a more extended sort of system that would transform the pair-of-forms P1-and-P2, for example, into the form p9, via the transformation "complement-of-union." I refrain from that exercise because I do not see how the added complexity of the new system would be justified by thus introducing the additional "forms" p4, p9, and Pt into the analysis.

operation of tritone-transposition. The tritone is a very prominent feature of the abstract P-pentachord. Furthermore, Stockhausen emphasizes the {2,8} tritone of m. 1 and the {e,5} tritone of m. 2 very strongly by temporal juxtaposition, register, and contour. Our network should be ready to assert any or all of the potential relations P6 = T6(P), P = T6(P6), p6 = T6(p), and p = T6(p6); on the network, the relations will be asserted by one-way or two-way T6-arrows connecting one node to another.

Inspecting example 2.2, we see that we will also want to assert some sort of "inversion" operation I that satisfies p = I(P), P = I(p), P6 = I(p6), and p6 = I(P6). We have several choices for "I" here. One of them is the operation that I call "inversion about A and B♭"; this is the operation that Forte (1973, 8–10) calls "inversion [about C = 0] followed by T7." I shall write "I7" as a synonym here. This operation is actually defined on individual pitch classes; given a pitch class whose number (on example 2.2) is n, the transformed pitch class has number $7 - n$. To perform I7 on a P-form, one simply performs I7 on each constituent pitch class of the pentachord.

The operation I7 does indeed transform P to p, p to P, p6 to P6, and P6 to p6. But I7 does not transform P8 to p8, or vice versa: I7(P8) is p4, not p8; I7(p8) is P4, not P8. Likewise, I7 does not transform P9 and p9 into one another; it transforms P9 into p3 and p9 into P3. And it transforms P2 into pt, and p2 into Pt. Thus I7 cannot be used to interrelate mutually inverted forms within our putative secondary complexes. Given the prominent secondary forms P8, and so forth, I7 does not group them together in complexes; instead it generates many P-forms that do not appear on example 2.2. The Forte inversion that maps P8 and p8 into each other, and that also maps P2 and p2 into each other, is not I7 but Ie. (Looking at mm. 8–10 on example 2.2, one can easily confirm that the various numbers of the p8-form are obtained when one subtracts the various numbers of the P8-form from eleven.)

There are ways of working around this problem.[6] However they

6. Those who are not interested should return to the main text at once. The key relationship is that Ie = (T8)(I7)(T4), where T4 is the inverse operation to T8. When

lead to a much more complicated sort of network than we seem to require here. What we are looking for is a way to use transformational discourse in rendering formal such intuitions as "P8 is to p8 as P is to p." The operation I7 will not do that trick, but a different operation will, an operation we shall call "J" for present purposes. Given a pentachord-form, J maps it into the unique form of the pentachord which inverts the given form and leaves invariant the four-note chromatic tetrachordal subset. Thus J(P) = p and J(p) = P. P and p are inverted forms of each other, and they share the same chromatic tetrachord {8,9,t,e}. One notes the determining relationship at once over mm. 1–2 on example 2.2 and again over mm. 5–8. Similarly, J(P6) = p6 and J(p6) = P6. P6 and p6 are inverted forms of each other, and they share the same chromatic tetrachord {2,3,4,5}. One notes this relationship too on the relevant portions of example 2.2.[7]

Now using the operation J as just defined, we can say what we could not say using I7 before: J(P8) = p8 and J(p8) = P8. For P8

one "modulates" from the 0/6 complex to the 2/8 complex, one can imagine the modulation accomplished by T8, transposing each form of the original complex by 8 to obtain the new complex. In this situation, the role of I7 with respect to the original system will be played by (T8)(I7)(T4) in the "modulated" system. The general theory of such situations is presented in section 6.7.2 of Lewin (1987, 147–49). Now, if SGP is some semigroup of transformations f, g, . . . on the family of P-forms, we can consider the transformations f' = (T8)f(T4), g' = (T8)g(T4), . . . on the same family. The transformations f', g', . . . form a semigroup SGP' of transformations-on-P-forms, and SGP' is isomorphic to SGP under the indicated correspondence of f with f', g with g', . . . We write f' = (T8)f(T4) = SGMAP(f), where SGMAP is the isomorphism just discussed. If f, g, . . . are transformations that we wish to assert within the 0/6 complex, then f', g', . . . will be the "analogous" transformations within the 2/8 complex. Hence the portion of our network that involves potential interrelations within the 2/8 complex can be made *isographic* to the portion that involves potential interrelations within the 0/6 complex. The relevant abstract theory is covered in sections 9.4.2 and 9.4.3 of Lewin (1987, 199–200).

7. The pitch class 2 of m. 1 is represented, in that measure of the music, by the lowest pitch heard through m. 10 of the piece. This makes it easy for a listener to articulate the opening P into the chromatic tetrachord (89te) in the upper registers, plus the odd-note-out (pitch class 2) in the bass. The pitch class e (eleven) of m. 2 is represented by a locally low pitch extremum as well, thereby articulating p6 of m. 2 in the same way as m. 1: chromatic tetrachord (2345) in the upper registers plus odd-note-out (pitch class e) in the bass.

and p8 are inverted forms of each other, and they share the same chromatic tetrachord {4,5,6,7}. This is clear over mm. 8–10 of example 2.2. We can also say that P2 and p2 are J-associates of each other; we could not make such a statement before using I7. This seems less urgent, since P2 and p2 are not concomitant — or even adjacent — in the time-flow of example 2.2. Still, given the intellectual idea of asserting a 2/8 complex, it is nice to be able to formulate the idea in transformational syntax. We can also observe that the non-adjacent forms p9 and P9 are J-associates — a convenient statement, given our earlier idea of organizing the two forms into a partial 3/9 complex.

We can make other trenchant statements using the J transformation. For example, the final two forms, Pe and p2, run virtually concomitantly. Earlier we observed that the pair Pe-to-p2 transposes the pair P6-to-p9 — that pair by which we left the original 0/6 complex of mm. 1–3. Using the J-transformation, we can write that $p9 = ((T3)J)(P6)$ and $p2 = ((T3)J)(Pe)$. Thus we assert the same transformational relation between p2 and Pe as between p9 and P6. We could not do this using I7: p9 does equal $((T3)(I7))(P6)$, but p2 does *not* equal $((T3)(I7))(Pe)$. As before, the problem with I7 can be worked around, but only by greatly complicating the conceptual apparatus.

Likewise, we can assert between the consecutive forms p5 and Pe (mm. 13–15) the relationship $Pe = ((T6)J)(p5)$. The equation suggests deriving the relationship from aspects of the referential 0/6 complex, where $P6 = ((T6)J)(p)$, $p6 = ((T6)J)(P)$, $P = ((T6)J)(p6)$, and $p = ((T6)J)(P6)$. This helps us view the pair p5-and-Pe as part of an incomplete 5/e complex analogous to the opening 0/6 complex. If we used I7, we would find the desired concepts much more difficult to express formally, since Pe does *not* equal $((T6)(I7))(p5)$.

Finally, the transformation J enables us to formulate a simply expressed transformational proportion involving the forms p9-and-P8 of mm. 2–5 and the forms P9-and-p8 of mm. 8–10. $P8 = ((Te)J)(p9)$; $p8 = ((Te)J)(P9)$. Actually, this is the proportion earlier suggested by the numerical notation for P-forms: because of the way in which we set up that notation, the forms Pn and pn will always be J-associates of each other. We should not let ourselves be seduced here by the elegant simplicity of the notation. As we saw earlier, p9-to-P8 preserves a common trichord {5,6,7} and replaces the tritone {2,8} of p9 with the tritone {4,t} of P8. P9-to-p8 is not fully "analogous" in the most intuitive sense: it also preserves a common trichord, {5,6,7}, but it juggles minor thirds rather than tritones; it replaces the dyad {8,e} of P9 with the dyad {1,4} of p8. So, while our proportion above is intellectually neat, we must be careful not to attribute to it any significance beyond what it actually asserts: Invert p9 so as to preserve its chromatic tetrachord and then transpose the result by interval eleven; the result will be P8. Invert P9 so as to preserve its chromatic tetrachord and then transpose the result by interval eleven; the result will be p8.

For some time now, we have been considering contextual operations of form ((Tn)J). It will be convenient to write such operations in a shorter notation.

Definition 1: The operation "Jn" is (for the present context) the operation ((Tn)J).

To apply the operation Jn to a pentachord form, one transposes by n the J-associate of that form, as indicated by the definition above: Jn(form) = ((Tn)J)(form). Let us apply Jn to the form Pk and see what happens. We transpose by n the J-associate of Pk; that is, we transpose by n the form pk, thereby obtaining p(k + n). We have demonstrated the first half of rule 1 below. The second half of rule 1 is demonstrated in similar fashion.

Rule 1: Jn(Pk) = p(k + n); Jn(pk) = P(k + n).

From rule 1, we can quickly derive rule 2.

Rule 2: JmJn = T(m + n). That is, for any k, JmJn(Pk) = (T(m + n))(Pk) and JmJn(pk) = (T(m + n))(pk). That is, applying Jm to the Jn-transform of any P-form yields the (m + n)-transposition of the given P-form.[8]

---

8. Proof: JmJn(Pk) = Jm(p(k + n)) via rule 1; this = P(k + n + m), again by rule 1; and this is the (m + n)-transpose of the given form Pk, (T(m + n))(Pk). In similar fashion, JmJn(pk) = (T(m + n))(pk).

Corollary 2A: The inverse operation to Jn is J($-$n).

The corollary follows from rule 2: combining Jn with J($-$n) yields the operation T (n $-$ n), which is T0, which is the identity operation on P-forms. Note that in general, the operation Jn is not its own inverse. The operations Jn behave very differently in this respect from the operations In: each In is its own inverse, meaning that (In)(In) = T0. In general, (Im)(In) = T(m $-$ n), not T(m + n).

Among the operations Jn, only J0 and J6 are their own inverses (since $-0 = 0$ and $-6 = 6$ mod 12). The two operations J0 and J6 are exactly those which we invoked, along with T6, in structuring our "complexes." Thus P8 and p8, for instance, are J0-associates (that is, J-associates) within the 2/8 complex; P2 and p8 (during mm. 10–12) are J6-associates within the same complex. p5 and Pe are J6-associates within the partial 5/e complex. We can use the locutions "J0-associates" and "J6-associates" because J0 and J6 are their own inverses. Thus if one P-form is the J6-transform of a second P-form, the second P-form is also the J6-transform of the first. That is, if form = J6(form'), then J6(form) = form'. We can not, however, speak of "Jn-associates" in the same sense, regarding a pair of forms, when n is not 0 or 6. In that case, if form = Jn(form'), it will not be true that form' = Jn(form). That is a strong difference in character between the Jn operations and the In operations.

We can characterize the effect of J6 as follows: J6 takes a pentachord form and inverts it so as to preserve the minor third of the form that is not filled in chromatically. For example, given the form {3,4,5,6,9}, J6 inverts it so as to make {6,9} the minor-third-that-is-not-filled-in-chromatically of the new form. Thus J6 applied to {3,4,5,6,9} yields {6,9,t,e,0}.

Corollary 2B: The J-operations commute, any one with any other.
That is, JmJn = JnJm.

The corollary follows immediately from rule 2, since m + n = n + m in modulo 12 arithmetic. Again we note that the J-operations behave very differently from the I operations under discussion; in general, two such I operations do not commute. Specifically, ImIn =

T(m − n) and InIm = T(n − m); the numbers m − n and n − m are generally not equal modulo 12. Rule 3 below tells us how the J-operations combine with transposition-operations.

> *Rule 3:* TmJn = J(m + n); also JnTm = J(m + n); any transposition commutes with any J-operation.

If so inclined, the reader may safely omit the proofs that follow. The first equation of rule 3 follows immediately from the definition of Jn: TmJn = Tm(Tn)J = T(m + n)J = J(m + n). The second equation of rule 3 follows from rule 1. Given the form Pk of the pentachord, JnTm(Pk) = Jn(P(k + m)); this is p(k + m + n), via rule 1. Again via rule 1, p(k + m + n) = (J(m + n))(Pk). In sum, JnTm(Pk) = (J(m + n))(Pk). Similarly, one demonstrates JnTm(pk) = (J(m + n))(pk). Thus, J(m + n) has the same effect on any pentachord-form as does JnTm. That is to say, JnTm = J(m + n) in the operational sense of equality.

The algebraic mechanics of our work on J-operations are summarized in the following structure theorem.

> *Structure Theorem:* The twenty-four operations of form Tm and Jn form a mathematical group of operations on the family of P-pentachord forms. The group is commutative. The operations combine according to the laws TmTn = JmJn = T(m + n);
> TmJn = JnTm = J(m + n).

Pursuing the implications of our methodological work so far, we shall use this group of operations in moving about within our analytic network for the piece.[9]

9. It is important to realize that the Jn are highly contextual operations; they operate on P-forms only, not on other pcsets or on individual pitch classes. This feature of the Jn operations stands in sharp contrast to the In operations, which can be applied to any pcsets or to individual pitch classes. We cannot apply the operation J0 (= J) to the individual pitch class Bb, for example; how are we to invert Bb into something that preserves "the four-note chromatic tetrachordal subset" of the single resulting note? Likewise, how are we to invert, say, a whole-tone scale "so as to preserve its chromatic tetrachordal subset"?

The remainder of this note is only for those who have dug pretty deeply into Lewin (1987). The group of the structure theorem is simply transitive on the family of P-

We have finally reached the all-important question: How are we to define a system of nodes and arrows within our network so as optimally to model the interrelations we want to assert among P-pentachord forms during the music?

At one extreme, we can make a system like that of example 2.4. Here we create a separate node for each distinct P-form "event" of example 2.2, and we use one-way arrows to move from earlier events of the piece to later ones. Two-way arrows are used only to interrelate events we judge to be completely "concomitant" in the acoustic time flow of the piece.

Example 2.4 has attractive features. With its many one-way arrows, it projects quite well the chronological progress of the piece through its various pentachord forms, indicating the "moves" between P-forms by T and J labels taken from the stipulated group of transformations. That makes it easy for us to read a strong narrative structure from the example, using the stipulated vocabulary. From the opening P, we move by J0 to p; T6 then takes us to p6, whence we again move by J0. That puts us at P6. From there J3 moves us to p9, whence P8 shunts off via Je. P8 is left temporarily hanging while we go back to pick up P6, one of the opening four P-forms. The piece briskly reviews all four of the opening forms together; thus we are exposed to a good deal of J0, J6, and T6 activity all at once. Abruptly this line of thought breaks off, and we return to pick up P8, which was earlier left hanging. The P8 is inflected by an immediately preceding p8, allowing us to hear the J0 relation in a new context.

And so forth. This blow-by-blow sort of analysis is common in the essays of enthusiastic music students at an early stage of their technical training. Nowadays, it is common as well in certain studies by sophisticated musical scholars, studies influenced by recent literary theories of narrativity. Surely one of the most powerful ways in which

---

forms: Given any two forms, there is exactly one operation in the group that transforms the first form into the second. It follows that the group can be used as a group of formal "intervals" to turn the family of P-forms into a (commutative) GIS. The group of Tm and In operations is also simply transitive on the family of P-forms, but it is not commutative. It would generate a non-commutative GIS, and that would be a much more complicated mathematical affair.

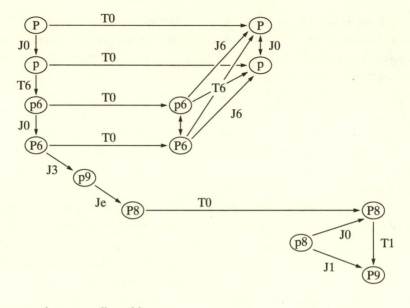

...and so on, ending with

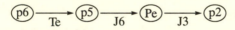

Example 2.4. A network whose left-to-right layout reflects the chronological progress of the piece through P/p forms.

we can make sense of our experiences conceptually is by arranging them so as to tell a good story.

And yet, despite the attractions of example 2.4, it has serious problems as well. Precisely because of the strongly narrative temporality, each arrow on the example has to bear enormous weight in asserting some sort of phenomenological presence. For instance, the Je arrow from p9 to P8 appears to assert not merely the possibility or potentiality of moving from p9 to P8 via Je in some abstract space defined or implied by the piece; it appears to assert as well the actual "hearing" of such a move at this moment in the listening process. But I cannot say that I "hear" the Je move as a presence. I cannot say even that I hear some specific "signature" of the move — a signature like the pivoting four-note chromatic cluster through which I can "hear" a J0-move from P to p in the music of mm. 1–2, or like the many tritones between the p-span of mm. 1–2 and the p6-span of m. 2, tritones that help me focus my aural attention — when I so choose — on the T6 move from the one form to the next. I hear nothing of the sort in the music to tell me I am hearing "a Je-move" in the middle of m. 5.

Furthermore, the structure of example 2.4 does not bring out well the proportional relations involving pentachord forms that led to our developing the T-and-J group in the first place. Given the example, we can certainly observe (if we so desire) that the Te-relation between p6 and p5 is the inverse of the T1-relation between P8 and P9. We can similarly observe that the J6-relation between p5 and Pe is the same as the earlier J6-relation between p6 and P, or that between P6 and p. We can similarly observe that the J3-relation at the end, between Pe and p2, is the same as the earlier J3-relation between P6 and p9. But the structure of the example does not draw our attention specifically to these proportions. To focus such attention, while we are telling the "story" of the example, we must interrupt the narrative drive.

In this respect the example does not reflect well the considerations and procedures that led to its own creation. The group of the structure theorem is not a list of immediate aural intuitions or intentions; rather it arose from our pondering the logic of global proportionings that emerged from careful reflection upon our overview. To be sure, we can ultimately try to refer these proportionings back to "presences," or at least observables, in the music. For example, we can aurally focus upon P8 in mm. 8–10; then we can aurally focus upon P9 in mm. 8–10; then we can hear the way in which our ear passes from P8 to P9. Next, we can aurally focus first upon P1 in mm. 9–11 and then upon P2 in mm. 10–11; now we can hear the way in which our ear passes from P1 to P2. Having done all this, we can finally focus upon the way in which the passage from P1 to P2 "sounds like" the passage from P8 to P9. To the extent that we succeed in our endeavor, we can say that we are "hearing" the effect of T1-proportioning "in the music." However, this sort of a posteriori ear-training is not at all the sort of "immediate aural intuition" we were discussing above.

Rather than trying to make our transformations denote phenomenological presences in a blow-by-blow narrative, we can more comfortably regard them as ways of structuring an abstract space of P-forms through which the piece moves. This sort of structuring is portrayed by the various visual motifs and parallelisms of example 2.5. The patterning of the example follows the sense of our earlier overview. The box at the upper left gathers together spatially the P-forms belonging to our "0/6 complex"; the box toward the lower right analogously gathers forms belonging to the analogous "secondary 2/8 complex". The two other boxes of the example organize forms belonging to the "incomplete 3/9 complex" and the "incomplete 5/e complex." Inside any box, a horizontal arrow always denotes a J0-

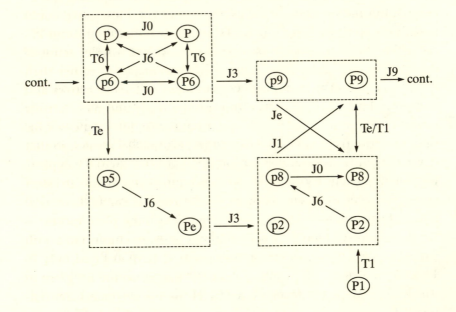

horizontal arrows within boxes = J0; between boxes = J3 or J9
vertical arrows within boxes = T6; between boxes = Te or T1
diagonal arrows within boxes = J6; between boxes = Je or J1

Example 2.5. A network that reflects a more spatial sense of pentachord organization.

relation, a vertical arrow a T6-relation, and a diagonal arrow a J6-relation. The "moves" J0, T6, and J6 are specially characteristic of complex-formation; the example makes the arrows corresponding to those moves shunt us about visually within whatever box we are in.

Between different boxes of example 2.5, a horizontal arrow always denotes a J3-relation or its inverse, a J9-relation. A vertical arrow always denotes a Te-relation or its inverse, a T1-relation. And a diagonal arrow denotes a Je-relation or its inverse, a J1-relation. All the characteristic moves of the piece are thus portrayed on example 2.5 by consistent visual motifs, bringing out the parallelisms which we observed earlier. Thereby example 2.5 — unlike example 2.4 — reflects very well the rationale that led to our developing the group of T-and-J moves in the first place.

It would be possible to augment example 2.5 by adjoining the P-forms necessary to complete the incomplete complexes. We could thus add more nodes on the map, to represent the missing forms P5, pe, p3, P3, and so forth. This recourse would give a fuller sense of the space in the example as a space of "potentialities" rather than "presences." That done, we could proceed to add more arrows and transformations as well. Indeed, we could already add more arrows to example 2.5 as it stands. Why not, for example, fill out the box for the 2/8 complex with all the possible J0, T6, and J6 arrows, so that the 2/8 box more completely resembles the box for the 0/6 complex? One might argue: Even if we do not intend the extra arrows to assert actual events in the music, we can surely assert them as theoretical potentialities in the P-form space through which the piece moves.

Despite the logic of this argument, I am more comfortable with example 2.5 as it stands. On the example, I have asserted only P-forms that actually appear "in the music," that is, on the list given in example 2.2. Also, I have drawn only such arrows as connect concomitant or reasonably consecutive forms on the same list. I am thereby conceding something, after all, to the spirit of blow-by-blow narrativism that underlies the extreme format of example 2.4. Some of this concession is essential, for the suggested augmentations of example 2.5, if pursued farther with complete logic, would lead to a model far more unsatisfactory than example 2.4. Such logic would tell us to draw a node for each of the twenty-four possible P-forms, any of which could "potentially" occur in the piece; by the same logic we would then continue, drawing from each node all twenty-three arrows to the other twenty-three nodes, since any of the possible T-or-J relations could "potentially" occur. Indeed, why not draw trillions and quintillions of additional nodes and arrows as well, to model all the further transformations that might "potentially" manifest themselves in the structure?

Clearly, our network must portray *some* actualities about the piece, not only to define but also to place bounds upon its potentialities. For my taste, example 2.5 as it stands is about right in this respect. It indeed shows a certain abstractly structured space of possibilities through which the piece moves, but it also shows how the abstract structuring is suggested and bounded by actual transitions within the progress of the piece itself.

But, one may ask, has not example 2.5 conceded too much toward the spirit of abstraction, ignoring the piece itself? On example 2.4, we can see very clearly "how the piece moves," but this is far from clear on example 2.5. True, example 2.5 does suggest correctly that the piece ends with a p2 form; but the example suggests as well that the piece begins with a p1 form — which is not so.[10] Additionally, example 2.5 does not show us how often we visit any of its nodes. Each P-form occupies only one node of the example; we cannot distinguish where the p6-form of m. 2 "is" from where the p6-form of mm. 5–7 "is"; nor can we distinguish either of these places from the location of the p6-form over mm. 11–13. Example 2.4 is very clear about such distinctions; there each pentachord-event of example 2.2 has its own autonomous node on the map. By and large, when we are at a node of example 2.4, we are at a particular *time* in an asserted *story* of the piece; when we are at a node of example 2.5, we are instead at a particular *place* in an asserted *space* of the piece.

That said, the big problem with example 2.5 comes into focus. To

10. Those familiar with Lewin (1987) will recognize a typical issue here involving "input" and "output" nodes. Such issues are discussed very lightly over sections 9.6 and 9.7 (pp. 207–19).

what extent is the example analytically useful beyond the most abstract level? To what extent can it engage the shaping of the piece as the music moves through chronological time? These questions bring us to the principal business of this chapter. I mean to show that a "spatial" network, such as example 2.5, can indeed engage the chronological temporality of the pertinent music in an analytically useful fashion. Of course it cannot do so completely by itself; it needs supplementation. We must study "how the piece moves," not simply in the raw acoustic time-flow, but specifically *through the space of example 2.5.* Example 2.6 will help us in that study.

The four parts of example 2.6 represent four different "passes" which the piece makes, chronologically, within the space of example 2.5. During pass 1 (example 2.6a) the piece moves from P to p to p6 to P6, exposing aspects of the 0/6 complex via J0, T6, and J6 arrows. Then the piece starts to modulate away from that complex, passing from P6 to p9 via a J3 arrow, and through the "pivot" p9 to P8 via a Je arrow. At the end of pass 1, then, the music has tentatively "modulated to the secondary 2/8 complex."

Now pass 2 begins (example 2.6b). It begins specifically with the onset of pitch class 4 in m. 5, where p6 and P6 forms both begin to recur; at the immediately subsequent pc t, forms P and p both begin to recur as well. This is the beginning of a new formal "pass," inasmuch as one cannot get directly from the P8 node of example 2.5 to the p6 or the P6 node of that example by following one arrow only, without traversing any intermediate nodes. One must, as it were, pick up one's pencil and set it down again to get from P8 to p6 or P6 on example 2.5. That is why pass 1 of example 2.6a ends at the P8 node, and pass 2 of example 2.6b begins afresh thereafter. Technically, there is a case for erasing some of the arrows on example 2.6b, since the p6 and P6 forms begin one pc earlier than the p and P forms, in m. 5. However, I have chosen to analyze all four forms as essentially concomitant here.[11] After studying the "modulation" of pass 1, we

11. I might also decide to start pass 2 at the p9 form of mm. 2–5; then I would adjoin, to example 2.5 and to example 2.6b, a J9-arrow from p9 to P6. That would still initiate a new pass, since there is no way to get from P8 to p9 on example 2.5 via

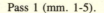

Pass 1 (mm. 1-5).

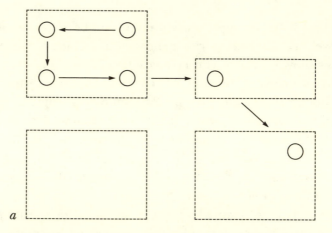

a

horizontal arrows within boxes = J0; between boxes = J3 or J9
vertical arrows within boxes = T6; between boxes = Te or T1
diagonal arrows within boxes = J6; between boxes = Je or J1

Pass 2 (mm. 5-8) goes back and elaborates
the beginning area of pass 1.

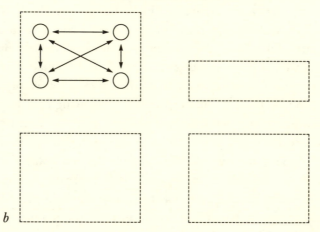

b

horizontal arrows within boxes = J0; between boxes = J3 or J9
vertical arrows within boxes = T6; between boxes = Te or T1
diagonal arrows within boxes = J6; between boxes = Je or J1

Example 2.6. The piece moves through the space of example 2.5 in four "passes."

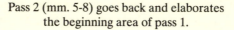

Pass 3 (mm. 8-10) picks up and elaborates
the ending area of pass 1.

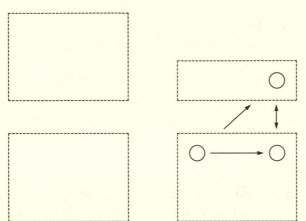

c

horizontal arrows within boxes = J0; between boxes = J3 or J9
vertical arrows within boxes = T6; between boxes = Te or T1
diagonal arrows within boxes = J6; between boxes = Je or J1

Pass 4 (mm. 9-16) expands the p8 + P8 area of pass 3
to activate P2 and p2 as well. P2 is the "essential" incipit
of pass 4; p2 is the end of the pass, and of the piece.

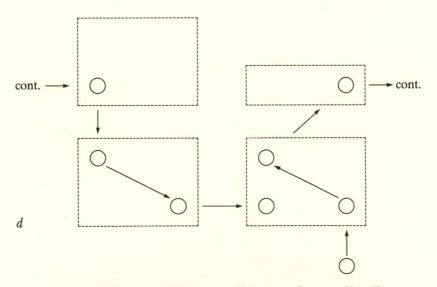

d

horizontal arrows within boxes = J0; between boxes = J3 or J9
vertical arrows within boxes = T6; between boxes = Te or T1
diagonal arrows within boxes = J6; between boxes = Je or J1

can attach certain significances to the gestures of pass 2 (example 2.6b). To use spatial parlance, they return to the tonic complex first marked by pass 1 and elaborate that complex. In temporal parlance, they return to the beginning of pass 1 and elaborate that beginning.

Pass 3 (example 2.6c) returns in the same senses to the secondary area marked by the ending of pass 1; it elaborates that area spatially and that ending temporally. The arrow-structure of example 2.6c makes it a bit tricky to speak of one formal "pass" here, but there are ways to make a suitable definition work.[12]

Pass 4, finally, proceeds according to the rationale expressed in the note to example 2.6d. The idea of "rationale" is important here. The events of pass 4 do not just turn over in haphazard narrative sequence; they transpire with a sense of overall meaning, executing a scheme one can infer from example 2.5 and 2.6a–c. The overall plan of pass 4 is to "start" at P2 and finish at p2, following an elaborate new chain of now-thematic T-and-J arrows. By marking P2 and p2 as the (essential) beginning and end of its action, pass 4 defines and attains a large goal, that of completing the 2/8 complex. The activity seems purposeful in the light of passes 1, 2, and 3. Because we can infer such a teleology, we can attribute a definite meaning to the idea that P2 is the "essential" beginning of the pass, even though P1 is its actual beginning. For we have a clear sense in which P1 can be regarded as formally "accessory to P2" in the larger context.

I find it useful to regard these matters as recapitulating in modern dress a traditional sort of interrelationship between *musica mundana*

---

one arrow only, without traversing intermediate nodes. The analytic decision here is less the point than is the technical apparatus that allows one to attribute significance to any such decision — that is, the technical apparatus that led us to example 2.5 and the supplemental theory of "passes."

12. Perhaps the easiest way would be to consider what I have called pass 3 not a formal pass but a conjunction of two concomitant formal passes. "Pass 3a" would proceed from p8 along the J1-arrow to P9 and thence along the Te-arrow to P8. "Pass 3b" would proceed from p8 along the J0-arrow to P8 and thence along the T1-arrow to P9. What I have called "pass 3" would then receive a different and special formal designation, as a certain sort of formal conjunction-of-passes. Alternatively, the formal definition of "pass" itself could be broadened to allow such a notion. I shall continue, in the main text, to speak of "pass 3" with these understandings.

and *musica instrumentalis*. The relations underlying example 2.5 exist outside human time in an abstract universe of quasi-spatial potentialities; they cannot be manifested in music except through human gestures that move through chronological time. On the other hand, the passes of example 2.6, which embody those sorts of gestures, might seem arbitrary or meaningless were not their contours and boundaries shaped by the abstract proportions of the given universe.

I now return to my main theme, the claim that examples 2.5 and 2.6 tell as good a story as did example 2.4. Indeed, I hold that examples 2.5 and 2.6 tell a better story, both because the sequence of events moves within a clearly defined world of possible relationships, and because — in so moving — it makes the abstract space of such a world accessible to our sensibilities. That is to say that the story projects what one would traditionally call *form*.

To be sure, we are not speaking of anything like "*the* form of the piece" here. The organization of examples 2.5 and 2.6 concerns only the succession of P-forms in the composition; it does not involve dynamics, note values, register, contour, and other such features as they may organize themselves autonomously or in conjunction with P-form structuring. Nor is it evident — certainly not to my ear — what the shape of examples 2.5 and 2.6 has to do with such matters. Still, I would find the results of our pentachordal study useful in preparing a performance, that is, useful as more than matters of abstract theory alone. Examples 2.5 and 2.6 enable us to articulate meaningfully at least one significant aspect of the piece; the examples further enable us to construct a story that links the meanings of the articulated sections in a coherent and consistent through-line. And that enables a performer, at every moment in the performance, to feel oriented with respect to such a through-line.

In this connection, I do not find it unduly difficult to focus my aural attention upon events in the music that I can associate with the story of examples 2.5 and 2.6. Example 2.7 helps communicate my feeling. The example blocks out the consecutive P-forms of example 2.2 as these are realized in register within the music. The single barlines of the example separate P-forms from one another; the double bar lines indicate the beginnings and ends of the four passes

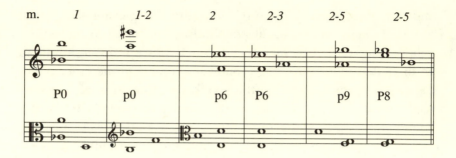

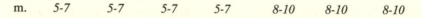

Example 2.7. An ear-training aid for listening to P/p forms and their inter-relations.

from example 2.6. Each P-form is displayed on example 2.7 as a chromatic tetrachord plus an odd-note-out.

To focus the ear upon matters at hand, I recommend the following agenda, which I have used myself with some satisfaction:

Play example 2.7 as a quasi-chorale; for each P-form sustain the chromatic tetrachord or odd-note-out, whichever comes first, through the subsequent odd-note-out or chromatic tetrachord. After thus playing example 2.7 a few times, continue to do so in alternation with the actual score (example 2.1). Quite soon the ear will pick up the asserted progression of P-forms within the piece, at least most of them.

Play pairs of important J0-related forms on example 2.7, hearing how the chromatic tetrachord is preserved in each case. The pairs include: P0 to p0 in mm. 1–2; p6 to P6 in mm. 2–3; P6 to p6 in mm. 5–7; P0 to p0 in mm. 5–7; p8 to P8 in mm. 8–10; P2 of mm. 10–11 to p2 of mm. 13–15. (The last of these J0-relations is not marked by an arrow on example 2.5, but it is useful to listen for it as it reflects part of the idea that P2 and p2 belong together in a secondary complex.) After listening to the J0-pairs on example 2.7, go over them again, relating each pair on that example to the sound of the corresponding music (example 2.1).

Do the same exercise for important T0-related forms on example 2.7: P0 in m. 1 to P0 in mm. 5–7 and so forth; also especially P8 in mm. 2–5 to P8 in mm. 8–10. The P8-to-P8 sound links the asserted end of pass 1 (example 2.6a) to the asserted beginning of pass 3 (example 2.6c).

Do the same for important T1-, Te-, J1-, and Je-related pairs. Listen, in each case, for the way in which the chromatic tetrachord of the first form is expanded to a chromatic pentachord when the second form follows. Listen for that particularly in comparing the effect of p9 to P8 (during mm. 2–5) with the effect of p8 to P9 (during mm. 8–10 and again during mm. 11–12).

And so forth for other constructive T and J relations. The chromatic tetrachord is a useful aural flag throughout. In moving from one P-form to another, if the chromatic tetrachord moves n semitones then the transformation involved is either Tn or Jn, and conversely.

I have traced my agenda at some length because I want to engage the typical questions one is asked about an analysis like that of examples 2.5 and 2.6: "Do you hear it?" "Can you hear it?" I take the question "Do you hear it?" to mean something like this: "On hearing the piece for the first time, would you infer at once the grouping of its pitches in P-form pentachords and the structuring of those pentachords as modeled by examples 2.5 and 2.6?" To this question I would certainly answer no, since I can answer the stronger (and clearer) question using the preterite instead of the conditional: *Did* I infer at once . . .? I did not. Nor do I think anyone should be expected to. I take the question "Can you hear it?" to mean something like this: After studying the analysis in examples 2.5 and 2.6, do you find it possible to focus your aural attention upon aspects of the acoustic signal that seem to engage the signifiers of that analysis? To this question I can certainly answer yes, and the above agenda fleshes out my answer. The exercise also shows, I think, that the question is not really very interesting. For me, the interesting questions involve the extent and ways in which I am satisfied and dissatisfied when focusing my aural attention in that manner. It is important to ask those questions about any systematic analysis of any musical composition.

I certainly feel more dissatisfactions about my own analysis here than I do say about a good analysis of a good piece by Beethoven. But that is not very surprising, even leaving aside the disengagement of my analysis thus far from dynamics, durational values, and so forth. If we demand that all music that we examine be on the aesthetic level of the great tonal masterworks, and that all the theoretical equipment we invoke be at the level of sophistication and power that tonal theory has achieved after two and a half centuries of intense development, we will not get very far in coming to terms with the music of our recent past.

This is not the place for an extended discussion of the satisfactions and dissatisfactions of a given analysis. An appendix to this chapter goes farther into the subject. Here let me recall one satisfaction noted in an earlier remark: "Examples 2.5 and 2.6 enable us to articulate meaningfully at least one significant aspect of the piece; the examples further enable us to construct a story that links the meanings of the articulated sections in a coherent and consistent through-line. And that enables a performer, at every moment in the performance, to feel oriented with respect to such a through-line." In this connection I group passes 2 and 3 together into one section 2; pass 4 is then section 3. The reason for this has to do with large rhythmic proportions. Given my reading, section 1 (= pass 1) takes up the duration of eighteen eighth notes; section 2 (= passes 2 and 3) takes up about 18½ eighths (overlapping its first 1½ eighths with the last 1½ eighths of section 1); section 3 (= pass 4) takes 22½, or 24, or 25⅙, or 26⅔ eighths, depending on whether or not one begins section 3 at the "accessory" E♭ of m. 9 or at the chord in m. 10 — also on whether or not one includes in section 3 the dotted eighth rest at the end of the piece. The "story" adhering to examples 2.5 and 2.6, given these rhythmic proportions, produces to some degree the effect of a traditional Bar form.

Let us return to the comparison of example 2.4 with example 2.5. Example 2.4 set out a blow-by-blow network for the analysis, a network that suggested a strongly narrative structure. Example 2.5, in contrast, set forth a spatial structure. Example 2.6 showed the results of "narrating" the piece on the spatial map of example 2.5. These ideas relate suggestively to studies in cognition by Jeanne Bamberger (1986).

Bamberger describes the procedures of various people in arranging a set of Montessori bells to play "Twinkle, twinkle, little star," in devising notations for scores to depict their spatial arrangements, and in devising (different) spatial arrangements to go with other people's (different) scores. There are eleven individual bells, specially cast so that they are indistinguishable by size, shape, or weight; the only way to tell one bell from another is to strike them with a beater. Eight of the bells form a C-major scale (including both low and high C); three other bells duplicate the low C, the E, and the G. Bamberger's paper focuses specifically on musically gifted children (identified as such by their performing abilities) aged seven to ten. Bamberger's project, however, also involves work with people of all ages and at all levels of musical talent and experience.

Bamberger contrasts the strategies of gifted seven-to-ten-year-olds arranging the bells with strategies adopted by two other groups. One contrasting group comprises musically untrained people, both children and adults. Such people consistently build what Bamberger calls a "figural" layout (p. 398). Example 2.8a (after Bamberger's figure 17.2, p. 398) shows this arrangement for the first two phrases of the tune; the arrows on the example show the path along which the piece moves through the layout. The untrained people construct the layout of example 2.8a methodically and systematically through the course of their work, adding one new bell to the right of their array as the "story" of the piece unfolds note by note.

Bamberger's other contrasting group comprises people with thorough "theory" training, no matter what their level of talent, eleven years old to adult. These people consistently build what Bamberger calls a "formal" layout (p. 399), shown on example 2.8b (after Bamberger's figure 17.3, p. 399). They proceed methodically and systematically, according to Bamberger, "by putting to themselves a previous task, namely, to 'put the bells in order' . . . by first ordering the mixed array of bells from lowest to highest . . . from left (low) to right (high). In short, they build a C-major scale. Once the bells have been thus ordered in their work-space, these subjects simply play the tune *on* the previously ordered set" (pp. 398–99).

Bamberger compares the strategies of the two contrasting groups with some salient remarks:

> As a result of their consistent and singular construction strategies, untrained and trained [older] subjects differ both in the bell-paths they make and in their action-paths on them. For untrained subjects, given a particular tune, it is the bell-path that is unique to the tune, the action-path [from left to right, one bell at a time] remaining constant

a figural layout (and path):

C———→ G———→A———→G———→F———→E———→D———→C

b formal layout (and path):

Example 2.8. Bamberger's figural and formal layouts and performance paths for configuring "Twinkle, twinkle."

across tunes. For trained subjects, given a particular tune, it is the action-path that is unique to that tune while the bell-path [from left to right in scalewise order, lowest to highest] remains constant across tunes. These strategies appear to be robustly consistent *within* the two groups. (p. 399)

Examples 2.8a and 2.8b can be compared pointedly with examples 2.4 and 2.5, respectively. Bamberger's "figural" layout for example 2.8a follows the events of the piece blow-by-blow; my "narrative" or "temporal" layout for example 2.4 comes close to this idea. Reading left to right across example 2.8 models the chronological succession of pertinent states in the music. The strong points of such layouts are their strongly narrative structures and their ability to recognize the difference in function between an earlier C or G (earlier P0- or P6-form) and a later C or G (later P0- or P6-form). Earlier and later events, even if involving the same bell (the same P-form) are at different places on the layout. Bamberger's "formal" layout for example 2.8b projects an abstract "spatial" arrangement of the various bells used; the layout for my example 2.5 approaches this idea with regard to the various P-forms used. In each case the spatial layout interacts cogently with a pertinent group of transformations. The linear arrangement of example 2.8b emphasizes the pertinence of the group comprising the transformations S_n on the scale, where S_n moves us "n steps" along the scale. By inspecting the arrows on example 2.8b, we can see at once just which S_n goes with each arrow: n is the number of places to the right that the arrow traverses on the example ($-n$ places to the right = n places to the left). The two-dimensional arrangement of example 2.5 emphasizes the pertinence of the group comprising the transformations T_n and J_n on the P-forms. By inspecting the arrows on example 2.5, we can see at once, to within a very small range of choices, just which T_n or J_n goes with which arrow; this feature is elaborated in the notes below the example.

The strong points of such layouts are their compactness, their ability to suggest the presence of pertinent group-structuring, and their recognition of "returns" within action-paths. Thus we can see that the action-path of example 2.8b "returns to its opening," whereas the action-path of example 2.8a ends at a maximum distance from its beginning. There is something of interest in each of the two observations, not just in the one concerning example 2.8a. Similarly the action of pass 2, in example 2.6b, "returns to the opening of pass 1 (example 2.6a)," while example 2.4 simply moves on to a new — and different — 0/6 complex at this moment. Again, there is something of interest in each of the two observations, not just in the one concerning example 2.4.

Thus, example 2.5 comes close to a "formal" layout in Bamberger's sense, and example 2.6 comes close to a series of "formal" action-paths in the same sense. Both examples make crucial concessions to a "figural" view as well. We noted such concessions earlier; it will be helpful to review them here.

First, not every one of the twenty-four potentially possible P-forms appears on example 2.5, only those forms actually referenced by the analysis. In contrast, example 2.8b lays out, *in advance of any analysis,* all the available pitch material at hand, as configured a priori by a pertinent group-structure. One notes in particular that example 2.8b configures the B bell and the high C bell with the others, even though these bells will not be referenced by the events of the piece at hand.[13]

Second, while example 2.5 is configured in a certain way to reflect the action of a pertinent transformation group on its elements, certain aspects of that group are emphasized over others by the choice of configuration. Specifically, the 0/6 complex and others are brought out visually; that is a result of an analytic decision to assign a primary role to the transformations J0 and J6, particularly J0. Indeed, the selection of a pertinent group was itself a contextual analytic decision here; we did not simply fasten on some available group to structure example 2.5 prior to investigation of the piece at hand. (If we had, we would have used the group of Tns and Ins, rather than developing our Jn transformations.)

13. One notes the effect of cultural conditioning here. A group of musically trained subjects in Europe around 1500 would not have included the B and high C bells. Indeed, Bamberger would not have reported the experiment in the same terms; the whole discussion would have referred to bells "ut," "re," "mi," "fa," "sol," and "la."

Third, while examples 2.6a–d are somewhat analogous to Bamberger's "formal action-path" on example 2.8b, there is a crucial distinction. On example 2.8b, any arrow between any pair of bells is a priori available when needed, via the pertinent Sn transformation. In contrast, examples 2.6a–d are constrained to use only the particular arrows that occur on example 2.5. In particular, we are not able to get directly from P8 to P6 or p6 (or P0 or p0) on example 2.5; no pertinent Tt or Jt (or T4 or J4) arrow is available to make that transit on the map. This is precisely what enabled us to define and articulate the beginning of pass 2 in our analysis. In general, were it not for such constraints on the arrow-structure of example 2.5, all arrows from any P-form to any other P-form would be equally available to us, each via the pertinent Tn or Jn transformation. In that case, the "formal action-path" of the piece through the map of extended-example-2.5 would perforce by completely continuous. We would never have to "pick up our pencil" while following the course of the piece on the map, and we would lose the pass-structuring that was such an interesting feature of our analysis.

So example 2.5 makes another important concession toward "figural" strategy in radically constraining the specific arrows available for use. As the reader will recall, the arrows on the example were selected not by a priori considerations (analogous to a C-major scale) but rather by analytic decisions of a "figural" nature. As I put it earlier, "I have drawn [on example 2.5] only such arrows as connect concomitant or reasonably consecutive [P-] forms on the . . . list [of example 2.2]." In sum, examples 2.5 and 2.6, while biased toward a "formal" (spatial) layout and action-path, make crucial concessions to "figural" (blow-by-blow temporal) considerations, and to that extent are mixed-mode constructions.

Furthermore, our constructive *strategy* was mixed, not just our eventual constructive mode. Whatever the layout of example 2.5, the *process* by which we got there involved an intermixture of "figural" and "formal" strategies. This bears on the title of the present chapter, "*Making* and Using a Pcset Network *for Stockhausen's Klavierstück III*." The reader will recall how, in making the network for our example 2.5, we first surveyed the figurally ordered list of P-forms in example

2.2. From that survey arose the idea of characteristic relationships that could structure a "space" through which the forms moved *in this piece*. That idea in turn led us to develop a group of transformations on the P-forms, a group *pertinent* to this piece. And that led us from the more or less "figural" (narrative) example 2.4 to a more "formal" (spatial) example 2.5. But example 2.5 made crucial concessions to narrative ("figural") aspects of the analysis — the concessions just reviewed. As a result, the "action-path" of the piece portrayed in example 2.6 differed crucially from a purely "formal" action-path (such as that of example 2.8b). In particular, the narrative ("figural") concessions of example 2.5 articulated example 2.6 into four discrete passes, a procedure that strongly asserted a particular form in the pentachordal progressions of the music.

Especially in the mixed-strategy aspect of our construction-process, and to a lesser extent in the mixed-mode aspect of our eventual layout, examples 2.5 and 2.6 can be usefully compared to the procedures and results of Bamberger's gifted seven-to-ten-year-olds. The most characteristic generality about their constructive procedures, she writes, is that *"shifts in strategy* [from figural to formal and/or vice versa] *occurred during the course of each child's work.* Further, with each strategy shift, priorities changed" (Bamberger 1986, 397, original emphasis). In fact, all the gifted seven-to-ten-year-olds began with a figural strategy: All of them arranged three bells in the configuration of example 2.9a (after Bamberger's unnumbered figure, p. 399). But then all of them abandoned a purely figural strategy precisely at the word "star" of the song, where the G "returns." Instead of adjoining the duplicate G bell to the right of example 2.9a, as in the purely figural model of example 2.8a, the children all recognized the note on the word "star" as a return to the "same place" as the note on the second word "twinkle." They reflected that recognition by a formal inflection in their action-paths, an inflection portrayed by the right-to-left arrow of example 2.9b (after Bamberger's first unnumbered figure, p. 400).

At this point, which Bamberger calls *"the critical moment"* (p. 400), the constructive strategies of the individual children diverged widely. But all strategies had in common the characteristic mix of formal and

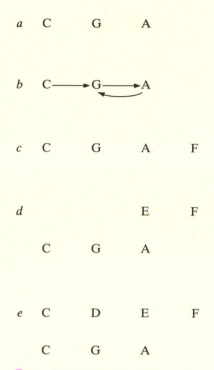

Example 2.9. Stages in the construction strategies used by Bamberger's gifted children.

figural motivations. The child Keith, for example, having reached example 2.9b, said "Backing up," moved his C-bell a space to the left, and inserted the F-bell to the left of the G-bell. He then iterated this procedure for the E-bell and the D-bell. In this way, he eventually arrived at the "formal" layout of example 2.8b. But his construction-*procedure* differed radically from that of the theoretically-trained people who constructed example 2.8b as an abstract C-major scale before beginning to analyze the piece. As Bamberger puts it, "Keith's low-high ordered series evolves *as a result of the particular structure of the tune and in the course of the construction process itself.* This is in marked contrast to the older [theoretically trained] subjects, who feel the need first to orient themselves by building the complete . . . scale. Only with the scale . . . 'in hand' are they then able to find the tune *on* it" (p. 401, original emphasis).

The child Rebecca, in contrast, having reached the critical moment of example 2.9b, continued as in example 2.9c (after Bamberger's table 17.2, move 4, p. 403), apparently abandoning the formal (spatial) idea that led her from example 2.9a to 9b and returning to a purely figural mode. But, upon trying to find a good place for the E-bell, she changed her mind about the F-bell and moved it from its position of example 2.9c to the new position shown in example 2.9d (after Bamberger's table 17.2, move 8); she then adjoined the E-bell as in example 2.9d. From there, she proceded to build her bell-configuration as in example 2.9e (after Bamberger's table 17.2, move 13). That configuration incorporates the idea of "passes" into the bell-arrangement itself: One cannot get from Rebecca's G-bell to her F-bell by any "Sn," that is, any pure leftward or rightward motion along n elements of a linearly-ordered array. (Nor can one get from her G to her F by simply proceeding consistently from left to right one bell at a time.) Her "pass" structure obviously reflects the phrase structure she hears in the composition — in the music or in the text or both. Example 2.9e thoroughly mixes Bamberger's figural and formal modes. Its bell-arrangement for the words "How I wonder what you are" is formal, not figural; left to right in this part of example 2.9e is from low to high along the C-major scale, not from one note of the tune to the next. As a result, Rebecca's second phrase does in some sense "return" to the place where the first phrase began — all the way to the left side of example 2.9e. On the other hand, Rebecca's arrangement also distinguishes sharply between the opening event of phrase 1 (the first "Twinkle") and the last event of phrase 2 ("are"); the events are modeled by different "places" on example 2.9e. That is a strongly figural feature of her arrangement. The sophistication of Rebecca's model involves her constructive use of two independent dimensions on the table-top where the bells were arranged.[14]

---

14. I am equally fascinated that Rebecca, having found the configuration of example 2.9e by working on the first two phrases of the song, continued to use the same arrangement for the next two phrases ("Up above the world so high / Like a diamond

I have discussed Bamberger's results at length because they fortify an important methodological point that I want to urge in connection with the construction of network-analyses. Specifically, I want to urge attention, at all times in the construction *process,* to both "figural" (narrative blow-by-blow temporal) and "formal" (abstract spatial) aspects of the task at hand. Such attention requires continual referencing of the models developed to the particularities of the piece being addressed. It also requires continual efforts to infer from those particularities a pertinent abstract space (or pertinent abstract spaces) of abstract potential "moves," a space (or spaces) through which the piece itself can metaphorically be sensed as "moving." The methodology of these ongoing processes, rather than the specific shape of this or that specific resultant network model, is what seems essential and characteristic in the art of *making* a network analysis.

Appendix

I said earlier that the interesting questions about "hearing" my analysis, for me, involve "the ways in which I am satisfied and dissatisfied when focusing my aural attention in that manner. It is important to ask those questions about any systematic analysis of any musical composition." To amplify the point, I shall discuss at some length here the analysis and methodological commentary for *Klavierstück III* offered by Nicholas Cook in a sensitive and highly practical study.

Surveying various formal and formalistic approaches to the piece, Cook (1987, 356) asserts that none of them "is going to tell us much about the way the piece is experienced." The passive voice is interesting. Cook (p. 354) includes among his surveyed approaches those of "some analysts" — he does not cite any — who "have seen this [piece] as all derived serially from the first five notes; but in order to do this you have to invoke transformations so complicated as to make the music's serial origins practically unintelligible." After his survey,

---

in the sky"; conversation with Bamberger). These phrases do not lie at all "naturally" on example 2.9e. Apparently the "A" section of the large ABA structure in the music took sufficient priority in Rebecca's ear that she was willing to continue using example 2.9e once she had determined it.

Cook continues more forthrightly in the active voice: "We have to think about what the music does to us rather than how it came about. We need to describe it rather than speculate about it" (p. 357). There follows a plausible and audible "way of chopping up the music into five sections" (p. 357), based mainly on the way in which Cook hears densities and registral contours working in different spans of the piece, which he hears as sometimes more polyphonic and sometimes less.

In determining and/or responding to his segmentation of the music, Cook adduces an eclectic variety of theoretical, cognitive, and intuitive considerations that he finds pertinent to his hearing here or there. For instance: "All pitch classes are used in this segment except C and D♭; that possibly suggests that some special role attaches to these notes"; ". . . the three sub-groups cohere because of the inverted arch shape that is outlined both by register and by . . . density"; ". . . there is a kind of rhyme [between certain chords] . . . simply because of their registral affinity, . . . [which] again helps to establish the three sub-groups as a single segment. But it is a very fragmentary one; for this reason it strongly implies continuation." ". . . the diminished-seventh chord [*sic*] in bar 11 seems to create harmonic implications of some kind"; because of the "diminished-seventh" — and also because of "a suggestion of three-part counterpoint," "conflicting shapes outlined by different parameters," and the lack of "clear overall shape either in dynamics or register" — we are to understand that a pertinent phrase "as a whole functions as a particularly distinct upbeat: imagine how unsatisfactory it would seem if the piece stopped here!" (pp. 358–60).

As the segmentation is being expounded, Cook develops the notion that its various "cadences", "fragmentary" aspects, "distinct upbeat functions", and the like, along with a "long term process of registral expansion," carry a sort of expectation-structure. "If the ending sounds conclusive, then, this is because it fulfils expectations established in the course of the piece as a whole; the music's form is to this degree organic" (p. 361). Cook then goes farther, attaching metric functions to his structure of expectations, so that "each [segment] seems to act as either upbeat or downbeat within the form as a whole.

Overall, the piece is directed toward its ending point . . ." From these protocols there eventuates a diagram of the sort employed by Cooper and Meyer (1960), applied to Cook's five segments. His segments I and II are represented as breves that move to a macron applied to segments III–IV–V as a bracketed group; within the bracket, segments III and IV appear as breves and segment V as a macron. Cook says of this metric diagram that it "simply expresses graphically the pattern of implications I described verbally earlier on . . . Above all, it demystifies the music; whereas the kind of 'cracking the code' approach I illustrated at the beginning of this section makes it seem remote and incomprehensible, more like some ancient magic spell than a living piece of music" (pp. 361–62).

My strongest satisfactions with Cook's exercise come from its being rich in what I earlier called "phenomenological presences." This makes Cook's reading of the piece easy to hear without special ear-training, given our present cultural upbringing; the attribute also makes it easy for us to "make sense of our experiences conceptually . . . by arranging them to tell a good story." Other satisfactions of a more particular sort come from his specifically addressing register and contour. Given the upwards move from A4 to B5 with which the piece begins, and the upwards move from A2 to B6 with which the piece ends — a move from the lowest to the highest note of the piece — one can hardly be satisfied with any analysis of the piece that does not address register and contour. And Cook's analysis is strong in just those respects, at least locally. I do have to strain to listen for his asserted "long-term process of registral expansion" that makes the "music's form . . . organic" in leading us to the ending (p. 361). When left to my own devices, I do not hear that the variations in local tessitura tell such an inexorable long-range story as he hears, nor do I always experience what seem to me rising tessiture as "registral expansions." Still, I do not find it difficult to focus my aural attention on what he asks me to, and my own pentachord-analysis is of course utterly dissatisfying as regards register and contour, about which it has nothing to say.

In general, my pentachord-analysis is dissatisfying in the same way with regard to all other aspects of the piece that it does not address.

Qua analysis, it needs supplementation. In some respects I feel similar dissatisfactions with Cook's work. For instance, I am keenly aware when I play the piece that there are exactly three dynamic levels for its notes, *p, mf,* and *f,* with the single exception of the last high B, which is *ff.* Cook's analysis, which does not engage this phenomenon, leaves me feeling all the more uncomfortable about what it means. Here I am more dissatisfied with Cook's analysis than with mine, because Cook asserts (p. 357) that he is describing "what the music does to us," whereas I am only asserting a rationale for the progression of its pentachord-forms (and an ear-training agenda to help one hear that progression).

I also have some dissatisfactions with Cook's manner of using received theoretical vocabulary and symbology to make inferences and to assert causalities. It would be one thing to say: "Listen to the arch-shape (diminished-seventh harmony, contrapuntal 'lines' that I have drawn, or whatever) during this passage; do you not agree, having done so, that you have this sort of intuition about the passage?" Cook's discourse takes what for me is an uncomfortable step beyond that, adopting a more "scientific" air of inferentiality that seems at best tenuous. For instance, "the three sub-groups cohere *because of* the inverted arch shape . . ." (Cook 1986, 360, emphasis added). What is being asserted by the specific discourse of causation here?

Do arch shapes create coherence in Stockhausen? In any art? For aesthetic reasons? Psychological reasons? The segment comprising the three sub-groups "is a very fragmentary one" and *"for this reason* it strongly implies continuation" (Cook 1987, 360, emphasis added). Does a sense of fragmentation necessarily induce a strong desire for continuation — for example, approaching the final cadence of Beethoven's *Coriolan* overture? Is the law here implicitly asserted a universal law of rhetoric? of music? of cognitive psychology? When I fall asleep, I often experience a sense of fragmentation in my conscious thoughts; does this "strongly imply continuation" of those thoughts? One would like to hear Descartes and Freud debate the question; I feel disinclined to express my own theories on the issue in advance.

To take another example "the registral shape of the segment . . .

is not the same as [the dynamic shape]; but both shapes coincide at the end and this *creates* a strong cadential feeling" (Cook 1987, 358, emphasis added). Does the coincidence of registral and (experienced) dynamic shape over the first four bars of *Coriolan* "create a strong cadential feeling?" Again, what is the law implicitly asserted, and what is it a law of? Coinciding shapes in any dimensions of anything? Of music? Specifically of dynamics and register in music?

From the E at the end of m. 2 through the G♭ of m. 4, Cook hears and urges us to hear two "linear motions" on his figure 178 (p. 359). One line goes E–G into m. 3 and one goes A♭–G♭ over mm. 3–4. I have no trouble focusing my aural attention on this, and I when I do so I have no trouble intuitively attaching the received term "polyphonic" to my response. I do, however, have trouble feeling any inference that *"because of* the linear continuity within each hand the effect is definitely polyphonic" (Cook 1987, 358, emphasis added). Among other problems, I don't know what he means by "linear continuity," a term he adduces in order to label the causative factor that he asserts. I suspect he wants me to listen to the E sustaining up to the attack of the G, and the A♭ sustaining up to the attack of the G♭. If so, why are these continuities specifically "linear" (rather than "acoustical" or something else)? What is the meaning of the technical term "line" in this context, particularly when the analytic job here is precisely to *articulate* two "lines"? If there is already "linear continuity" (p. 358) before two lines arise "because of" the "linear continuity," what is the sense of the inferential, causative parlance?

I relate this sort of dissatisfaction about Cook's discourse to a dissatisfaction I have with some of his asserted shapes, where I feel a need for some support in asserting those shapes but not others. For example, over mm. 5–7 Cook's figure 178 asserts a chiastic voice-leading. It specifically asserts two "linear motions"; one descends from E in m. 5 through B♭ and D to A in m. 7; the other ascends from F in m. 5 through D to G♯ in m. 7. In this reading, the B and E♭ of m. 6 do not participate in any "lines." The omission of B and E♭ might just be a defect in the set-up for Cook's figure 178; B might be supposed to participate in the descending line and E♭ in the ascending one. In any case, the overall assertion of chiasmus is clear, and Cook refers to it as a self-explanatory "contrary-motion expansion of register" (p. 358).

But I fail to hear how Cook's register "expands." Over mm. 5–7, the soprano moves overall up four semitones, from E to G♯; the bass moves overall in parallel motion, up four semitones from F to A. Why not speak of a "rising tessitura"? Presumably, Cook might be able to explain more precisely what he hears "expanding" in this context. Possibly, though, he joined a sense of "rising" in the soprano (or in the overall tessitura) with a sense of "chiasmus" in the registral voice-leading, and arrived via an erroneous metaphorical equation at a sense of "expansion."

This is no small matter, since Cook continues: "There is a very definite sense . . . specifically that the registral expansion . . . will be completed later on" (p. 358). And, later on, the ending of the piece "provides the expected conclusion to the long-term process of registral expansion . . . it fulfils expectations . . . the music's form is to this degree organic" (p. 361). In Cook's hearing, the all-important "process of registral expansion" begins precisely at his chiasmus of mm. 5–7.

A second problem is with the chiasmus itself: I do not hear it as self-evident, as Cook apparently does. Why should I prefer Cook's voice-leading here to other possibilities, say, to hearing a sort of contour mirror-crab between E–E♭–G♯ in a "soprano line" and F–B–A in a "bass line"? I have no trouble focusing my aural attention on that if I wish, supplying some quiet clarinets or horns to fill in the harmony on B♭ and D. If I were to prepare a legal brief on behalf of Cook's hearing, I could argue that the large unidirectional contour-sweeps in Cook's chiastic "lines" for mm. 5–7 develop consistently the large unidirectional contour-sweeps of mm. 1–2, contours which can be asserted as thematic. This is all well and good, but why do we want to hear thematic development, in this respect, over mm. 5–7? Why don't we want to hear thematic contrast during this passage, with its three-note chords? If we are so biased toward hearing large unidirectional contours as thematic, what is there about the previously analyzed "polyphony" of mm. 3–4 (with pickup) that overrides the "linear continuity" of a putative large unidirectional gesture sweeping up from E in m. 2 through (the immediately ensuing) A♭ in m. 3 to G♭ in m. 4? The two-note chord in m. 3 could suggest such an override, in some way. But in what way? Should we assign a special "second-group" sort of thematic function to simultaneities in the piece, in this connection? Then again, if the simultaneity of m. 3 creates registral "voices" when Cook listens, why do the simultaneities of m. 5 and especially m. 7 not create similar registral parts, leading to my "soprano line" and "bass line" posited there? These important aural explorations are sidestepped by asserting, a priori, a self-evident "contrary-motion expansion of register" over mm. 5–7.

Actually, when I try listening to Cook's chiasmus, what I become most aware of is a retrograde relation in the time-span structures of mm. 5 and 7. Measure 5 packs together three notes that last a dotted quarter, a dotted eighth, and an eighth, respectively; the packing is structured so that the three time spans release simultaneously at the end of m. 5. Measure 7 also packs together three notes that last a dotted quarter, a dotted eighth, and an eighth, respectively; here, however, the packing is structured so that the three time spans attack simultaneously (downbeat of m. 7). The loose sense of palindromic structuring over mm. 5–7 in this respect seems to interact nicely with Cook's sense of registral chiasmus, though there is hardly any question of necessity or causation; the palindrome works equally well with my loose mirror-crab in the outer voices.

Sometimes I feel other dissatisfactions about Cook's verbal descriptors. Certainly, to the extent that we are being asked merely to listen to various things, and to put together some impressions about those things in intuitively resonant ways, it does not make sense to demand a great deal of precision in the terms used for description. However, it does seem to me that Cook's relaxed discourse from time to time sidesteps analytic/aural issues one would like to confront. For example, he says of mm. 11–12 (with pickup) that "there is no clear overall shape either in dynamics or register" (p. 360). What is a "clear overall shape"? Is "clear" a synonym for "unidirectional," with regard to dynamics or register? If so, why not say so, and point our listening much more precisely and helpfully? If not, what other shapes are abstractly "clear," or would be contextually "clear" at this point in the piece? An arch shape, perhaps? I am not picking nits; it is possible in this piece to assert a particular thematic priority for unidirectional registral contours, and it is also possible to avoid asserting such a thematic function for such gestures. Where are we standing on the analytic/aural issue? Are we listening thematically at all? If so, are we listening for unidirectional contours as specific thematic elements? One does not quite know.

The problem with descriptors becomes more intense when Cook begins to introduce the word "upbeat" in contexts where he is suggesting that we explore feelings of implication or expectation. Regarding mm. 11–12 (with pickup), Cook points out what he regards as complexity caused by "a suggestion of three-part counterpoint [introduced into a less contrapuntal texture]" and "conflicting shapes outlined by different parameters." He then talks about the lack of "clear overall shape" in dynamics and register. Then he mentions a tonal response that he has (and I share) to the "diminished-seventh chord [*sic*] in bar 11." His discussion of this passage concludes: "The effect of all this is that the phrase as a whole functions as a particularly distinct upbeat: imagine how unsatisfactory it would seem if the piece stopped here!" (p. 360).

I have problems with the word "upbeat" as a descriptor for a phrase as a whole, in an essay where Cook has said he is going to "describe . . . rather than speculate" (p. 357). Is it a criterion for detecting a "particularly distinct upbeat" that a listener would find it "unsatisfactory . . . if the piece stopped" there? Is the beginning of the last movement in Beethoven's Ninth Symphony a particularly distinct upbeat? The first chord of the First Symphony? The *Eroica*? The sonority on the downbeat of m. 3 in the *Eroica*? Apparently the upbeat function of a phrase-as-a-whole is an *effect,* brought about by some cause or causes. Here the causes are, according to Cook, "all this." But surely that is overkill, and too relaxed besides. In what way does each of the causes advanced contribute to the effect asserted? Indeed, *do* they so contribute as a matter of theoretical principle, and as a matter of description, not speculation? *Does* a "phrase as a whole" function more "as a particularly distinct upbeat," to the extent that there is more contrapuntal complexity than in the preceding phrases?

Is the opening phrase of the first Agnus Dei in Palestrina's *Pope Marcellus* Mass to that extent a particularly distinct upbeat? The opening phrase of the second Agnus Dei? And so forth for each of the other "causes."

As the word "upbeat" acquires heavier and heavier baggage in Cook's text, I become more and more restless. In what sense can one say that a Cooper-Meyer graph, of nested breves and macrons adhering to spans of a piece, "simply [*sic*] expresses graphically" a "pattern of implications" (Cook 1987, 361) already discussed verbally? (The earlier discussion refers to "expectations," not "implications"; Narmour (1977, 136–37), criticizing Meyer, sharply distinguishes the two concepts.) Is "upbeat" synonymous with "expectation" here, or with "implication"? What is the meaning of "simply"? Is it a simple matter to bring a Cooper-Meyer sort of rhythmic theory into the context of *Klavierstück III,* and then to claim that this usage is descriptive, not speculative? Cook asserts of his breve/macron graph that it "clarifies something about the way this piece is experienced" — presumably something beyond his earlier verbal intuitions of expectation or implication. "Above all," says Cook, the graph "demystifies the music . . ." I can see the sense of his asserting that his ideas about expectation can help an intimidated student feel more at ease with the music. But I cannot see how the abrupt incursion of Cooper-Meyer rhythmic symbols into this context demystifies anything. Quite the contrary, the symbols confuse me. Why do we need them? Why is their code better than other codes against which Cook immediately inveighs? Because Cooper-Meyer rhythmic theory is correct and natural, unlike all other rhythmic theories — those of Hauptmann, Riemann, Komar, Lester, Lerdahl and Jackendoff, Lussy, Westphal, Yeston, and so on through a myriad of others? Because a Cooper-Meyer breve/macron graph is somehow not an encoding?

Still, I find all these dissatisfactions regarding the ways Cook uses technical concepts and symbols to be relatively minor annoyances. Many of them could be eliminated, without substantially changing Cook's reportage, by a more concentrated and careful discourse. There remain more general dissatisfactions with Cook's approach, and these disturb me more. They arise from the notion, implicit within much of Cook's discourse and explicit in some of it, that we can afford to bypass any special effort to focus our ears on things about the piece that might not lie at hand from our previous musical training and experiences. I am disturbed because the most crucial critical demand I make upon my experience of an artwork is that it make me undergo again Rilke's experience before the torso of Apollo: "Du mußt dich ändern." The quality of the conviction, not its intensity or extent, is the crux of the matter; if the world is not in some way sensibly different as a result of the artistic deed, then I do not see in what sense one can say a work of art has transpired. In reading Cook's story of the piece, I get too much of the message, "Du mußt dich nicht ändern." I get the message that I can be perfectly at home with my listening if only I listen in a common-sense fashion for contours and registers and densities, and apply to those experiences some casual inferences from received notions about arch shapes, upbeats, etc. In this way I will hear that (and how) Stockhausen's piece, except for quirks in its notation, is quite traditional and comfortable; it will not challenge me, or provoke me, or in some ways infuriate me. I can see the point of encouraging inexperienced students to listen freely and to trust their ears at any stage of their training. But Stockhausen's piece does challenge me, and provoke me, and in some ways infuriate me, and make me want to extend my hearing — and that is precisely one of the most vital things it does to me. So I feel dissatisfaction at an analysis that does not make me extend my ways of listening, and I feel it all the more when the analysis tells me pointedly that it is setting out to describe "what the music does to us."

I doubt that Cook would have much patience with my network analysis; I suspect he would read it as yet one more exercise in what he calls "cracking the code." Let me be the first to say emphatically that the network analysis is very far from an analysis of the piece, that I find it problematical, and that it took some effort for me to develop the aural agenda of example 2.7. However, I must say that I enjoyed developing that agenda, which of course I did gradually as my work developed, and not in so neatly packaged a way as in this essay. I felt I was getting at something in the piece that very much involved "what the music did to me," if only in one of its aspects. I felt I was responding in some measure to a strong sense of challenge I felt about the piece. No matter to what degree I am deluding myself, I miss in Cook the sense of *having* to extend my ear in response to a sense of challenge.

"We need to describe" the piece, writes Cook, "rather than speculate about it." Well and good in an obvious sense. But the sentiment does not stand up quite so well if one digs at it. The implication is that we already have at hand all the conceptual tools we need to "describe" the piece. Elsewhere Cook is more explicit on that notion: "in general I think that our present analytic techniques are rather successful" (p. 3). He allows early music as an exception, but apparently not music since 1945. The anti-theoretical stance becomes, I think, too extreme to be quite tenable. Is the concept of "subdominant" something that can be used to "describe" certain musical sensations, or is it "speculation" about music? Today? In 1727? Does the date make a difference, and if so, what is the difference? Is the concept of "middleground Zug" something that can be used to "describe," or is it "speculation"? Today? In 1931? Does the date make a difference? Is the concept of "mode" something that can be used to "describe"? How about "upbeat?" "Implication?" And so forth. Such terms are not just "there" in the language; they got *put* into the language at definite times with definite rationales, many of which were (and still are) arguably highly speculative. Are we free to use the words of Pietro Aron, Rameau, Riemann, Schenker, Cooper-Meyer and others today as purely "descriptive"? Are we somehow not free to develop new concepts in the same way that earlier writers were, if we feel ourselves confronting new musical sensations? Has history stopped?

Cook's reference (p. 360) to the vertical sonority in m. 11 as a "diminished-seventh chord" points the issue. In what way is an E in the bass, carrying its major sixth C♯ and its minor tenth G above it, a "diminished-seventh chord"? Would one refer to the sonority in Palestrina or Lassus using that name? If not, why is one free to use the name in Stockhausen? Is the absent diminished seventh of the "diminished-seventh chord" necessarily implied, even in Mozart or Chopin? Why does Stockhausen's chord function more as a "diminished seventh" than as a certain characteristic trichord within the P-harmony? Because we are familiar and comfortable with the 250-year-old term, so we will not have to exert our ears?

My dissatisfactions are even more sharply pinpointed by a few short remarks Cook makes at the end of his discussion about Stockhausen's rhythm. The "precise mathematical notation of rhythms," says Cook,

> encourages numerological rather than musical analysis. But musically Stockhausen's rhythmic notation is a kind of science fiction: what actually happens is that the performer improvizes the rhythms more or less in accordance with Stockhausen's specifications, and the result is a rhythmic fluidity and independence of any fixed beat that probably could not have been easily achieved in any other way. In other words there is a glaring discrepancy between the fearsome mathematical complexities of *Klavierstück III's* [*sic*] notation . . . and the way in which the music is actually performed and experienced by the listener. (pp. 362–63)

Once again: as a device for making an inexperienced student less anxious, the passage is understandable. It is also understandable as a musicological generalization about certain pieces by Stockhausen; Cook refers to other piano pieces not mentioned in the quotation. What disturbs me, and particularly so in a book entitled *A Guide to Musical Analysis*, is the sense of giving up in advance on the rhythmic problem in the particular piece at hand, retreating into musicological generality without even an effort to extend the rhythmic ear. I find only two rhythmic details of the piece really hard to play, and one passage moderately hard. Really hard are the releases on the tied thirty-second note of m. 10 and on the isolated quintuplet thirty-second C♯ of m. 11. The difficulty lies not so much in the mathematics of counting, as in damping the instrument's sound cleanly at the indicated times. Moderately hard is the rhythm of m. 15 following that of m. 14; this, however, responds to practice.

For those to whom the rhythmic notation of the piece may seem a "fearsome mathematical complexity," I suggest the following ear-training agenda. Set your metronome at a comfortably slow beat; I suggest MM.=54. Now get yourself clapping accurately at a rate of six claps per tick of the metronome. After keeping that going for a while, try to change instantaneously to a slightly slower rate, so that you are making exactly five claps per tick. You will probably either undershoot or overshoot the desired rate on your first try. If so, do not stop clapping; rather, move back at once to your six-clap rate and settle into it again. Now make another try for the instantaneous change to a five-clap rate. You will do better. (You may be pleasantly surprised by how much better you do.) If you have not yet got the relation fixed internally, go back to the six-clap rate, reestablish that, and then try for the five-clap rate again. And so forth. Eventually — probably sooner than you suspect — you will be able to move back and forth with confidence between an exact six-clap rate and an exact five-clap rate.

Now practice the following, with the metronome ticking: a group of six claps and a group of five claps, a group of six and a group of five, and so forth. When you have got that down, do the same exercise, only now focus special attention on the fourth clap of each five-clap group, without making any dynamic accents. Now turn off the metronome, go to the piano, and play m. 1 at a constant dynamic level, using your metronome beat as half the measure. The last attack of the measure, the high A, comes on the fourth clap of the five-clap group.

Now leave the piano and turn on the metronome again. Clap in tempo the attack times of the first note in m. 1, the last two notes of m. 1, and the first note of m. 2 (that is, the first beat of a six-group, the first and fourth beats of a five-group, and the following tick). When you have that rhythmic example internalized, reset your metronome to exactly twice the tempo and clap the attacks just mentioned *doppio movimento*. When you have that down, go the piano and play m. 11, beginning with the three-note chord, cheating on the duration of the C♯ as much as is comfortable. When you have that down, practice all of m. 11.

The transition from m. 14 to m. 15 is more difficult. Partly that is because the relation of six claps to seven claps is harder to internalize than that of six claps to five claps. I think this is mainly because the music over the first half of m. 1 provides a good "six claps" for our ear, while there is nothing in the music of m. 14 to subdivide its one attach into "six claps."

Those who go through this ear-training agenda will, I think, share my dissatisfactions with the idea that "there is a glaring discrepancy between the fearsome mathematical complexities of *Klavierstück III's* [rhythmic] notation . . . and the way in which the music is actually performed and experienced by the listener." At least they will appreciate those dissatisfactions so far as performing this piece is concerned. While I am analyzing this piece I do not care about generalizations that might be true for other works but not for this one. In any case, I suspect Cook's generalizations about Stockhausen's rhythms. The question is not whether a given rhythmic proportion can be performed with mathematical exactness. The arithmetically simpler proportions of Baroque and Classical music are not performed in that way, any more than are the more complex proportions of Stockhausen. Rather, the question (in each case) is: Can a clear rhythmic conception be projected by the performance? My remarks elsewhere on *Klavierstück I* speak to that issue (Lewin 1991, 126–29).

Cook's "the listener" gives me somewhat different dissatisfactions. I have always had trouble visualizing this person as distinct from the particular individual who is speaking. Irony aside, there is a real issue here. I find it hard to imagine people who have not already internalized the rhythms of Stockhausen's piece being able to catch those rhythms by listening alone. I respond to that, however, as a problem in the sociology of music rather than its analysis. I cannot imagine the propriety of imposing forced ear-training on such listeners, or of forbidding them to listen to the piece. On the other hand, I do not see any reason for valuing their aural inabilities over the aural abilities of trained musicians in a specific context where one professional musician or student is talking of analysis to another. Would we so specially value deficiencies in the responses to a Monteverdi madrigal of listeners who had never sung in a vocal ensemble? Or the responses to a Haydn quartet of listeners who had never played chamber music?

I can certainly see the propriety of using listeners' problems as the basis for a negative critique of Stockhausen in general, or of a specific Stockhausen piece. But negative criticisms of a piece one is analyzing hardly advance the analytic project at hand; if one believes a piece to be seriously flawed aesthetically, why devote great care to its analysis? (And clearly Cook likes this piece; his enthusiasm is engaging and attractive.)

No doubt Cook, if he went through my ear-training agenda, would internalize perfectly well the durational proportions I have just discussed. I imagine he would find the experience sterile, abstract, and pointless (where I find I am hearing more and better "what the music does to me"), but that is another matter. My dissatisfaction lies not in such disagreements but in the overall tone of his message on the "fearsome complexities." The message is that one might as well abandon — in advance of any attempt — the notion of possibly being able to extend one's ear to focus with some clarity upon rhythmic features of the piece that at first seem unfamiliar.

All this said, if I were a pianist with little exposure to Stockhausen trying to work my way into *Klavierstück III*, I would rather use Cook's analysis as a point of departure than mine. It addresses in a tangible way features of the piece that are much more "phenomenological presences." And the sorts of dissatisfactions I feel about it are such as to stimulate further thought, by way of response, about the phenomenology of the music. My network analysis might come into play at a later stage of familiarity with the music, should a person develop — as I did — a sense that there is an overall story to be told in the establishment of a certain consistent harmonic field for the piece, and in the progression of the piece through that field. The differences in segmentation between Cook's analysis and mine should not be problematic, I think, except for those who believe that form is "a Form," something a piece has one and only one of in all of its aspects.

CHAPTER 3

Set Theory, Derivation,
and Transformational Structures
in Analyzing
Webern's Opus 10, Number 4

Forte (1973, 89–91) discusses this work in connection with the methodology of segmentation. He articulates the piece into "three sections, separated by rests in all parts," and notes that "only one set occurs in all three sections: 6–Z43." Example 3.1 lays out the pitches of the music roughly following Forte's examples 93–94. I have represented the rests between Forte's sections by commas in place of his bar lines. The forms of 6–Z43 that he cites are marked on my example as H = {C,D♭,D,F,G♭,A♭}, T9(H), and L(H), where L denotes inversion about D or about A♭.

Forte points out that within T9(H) the first five pitch classes B♭–A–B–F–E♭ project melodic interval classes {1,2,2,6}, and that atop L(H) the final melodic gesture A♭–B♭–E–D–E♭ also projects melodic ics {1,2,2,6}.[1] Forte does not follow his commentary through to the

---

1. The correspondence between melodies is in fact much stronger; we shall explore

Example 3.1. Webern, Orchestral Piece, Op. 10, No. 4: H, T9(H), and L(H) appear at specially marked places in the composition.

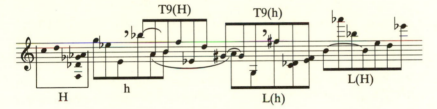

Example 3.2. H, T9(H), L(H), and their complements cover all notes of the piece in three (pseudo-) aggregates.

sort of analysis one finds a bit farther on in his book, after he has introduced his theory of set complexes, but he evidently believes that the forms of H are strong determinants for the pitch-class structure of the composition.

He is right. It is not necessary to assign such great priority to the rests as articulators of form. H (as seen on example 3.1) comprises the first six notes of the piece, while L(H) comprises the last six. The Bb5 that begins T9(H) occurs not only after a rest in all parts but as a prominent local climax in the registral contour. Furthermore, the three cited hexachord forms interact cogently with total chromaticism. Example 3.2 elaborates that idea.

---

the matter later. As we shall see, Forte is especially perspicacious in drawing attention to this pentachord not simply at the end of the piece but earlier as well.

The complement of H is labeled h = {3,4,7,9,10,11}, a form of 6–Z17. The notes of h follow right after the notes of H to build an aggregate. The notes of T9(h) likewise follow right after the notes of T9(H) to build an aggregate. In T9(h) one must ignore the repeated A4 of example 3.2; the G♯ is attacked after the (first) A. Finally, the notes of L(h) "precede" the notes of L(H) to build a pseudo-aggregate. In L(h) one must count the opening A4 but not the G♯; one must also hop over the E4, in moving from L(h) to L(H). These maneuverings are awkward, but to some extent they can be rationalized by appealing to the idea that the hopped-over G♯ and E are being "counted" by T9(h).

The point of example 3.2 is that the three H forms, together with their corresponding h forms, reference every note of the composition. A certain strain is evident in asserting L(h), to be sure, but not so much as to destroy the force of the observation. h = {3,4,7,9,10,11} = {S,E,G,A,B,H} is a siglum set for A.SHBEG. That is amusing, if probably only coincidental.

Various other forms of H and h can be found in the piece; we shall explore most of them later. Example 3.3 beams one of them, the form I(H) comprising six notes in the upper register at the beginning. "I" here signifies inversion about E or about B♭. Why should I(H) be specially highlighted on example 3.3? According to the set-theoretical analysis given up to this point, we can view the H-structure

Example 3.3. The piece is almost completely covered by four H-forms, plus the axis tones for the inversions that relate consecutive forms.

of the piece as moving from H to T9(H) to L(H); why do we need
or want I(H) in the picture? The answer is that a much more convincing transformational story of H-forms comes across when we view
the basic H-structure as moving from H through I(H) to T9(H), and
thence to L(H).

Example 3.4 graphs the story, using arrows labeled I, J, and K.
"I", as before, signifies inversion about E or about Bb; the I-arrow
means that I(H) is the I-inversion of H. "J" signifies inversion about
Eb-and-D, or about A-and-G#; the J-arrow means that T9(H) is the J-
inversion of I(H). "K" signifies inversion about G-and-F#, or about
Db-and-C; the K-arrow means that L(H) is the K-inversion of T9(H).
One notes that the tessiture of the four H-forms rise from H to I(H)
to T9(H) to L(H). We shall soon see how well the I,J,K progression
of example 3.3b works out as a transformational analysis.

On example 3.3, the I-relation between H and I(H) can be heard
by focusing upon the disposition of pitches in register. The opening
melodic C5–D5 is answered by {Gb4,Ab4}, the inversion of {C5,D5}
about Bb4. Then the Db4 of the chord is answered by the melodic
G5, the inversion of Db4 about Bb4. Next the F3 of the chord is
answered by Eb5. If the Eb5 were Eb6, the inversion about Bb4 would
be perfect. As it is, the Eb5 is an I-partner for the F3, but only a
pitch-class partner. The pitch center of the F3-Eb5 dyad is E4, not
Bb4. E4, indeed, will be the next note of the piece to sound. In sum,
all the pitches of H, on example 3.3, balance all the pitches of I(H)
by inversion about Bb4, except for the lowest pitch of H and the last
pitch of I(H). Later we shall explore other sorts of audible I-struc-
turing in this passage.

Immediately following on example 3.3, E4 and Bb5 appear with
open noteheads. Each of those pitches is a center for the pitch-class
inversion I; together, the pitch classes E and Bb constitute an axis for
the pitch-class inversion. The axis notes bridge the comma, articulat-

$$H \xrightarrow{\ I\ } I(H) \xrightarrow{\ J\ } T9(H) \xrightarrow{\ K\ } L(H)$$

Example 3.4. The basic transformational
progression for H-forms.

71

ing the end of Forte's first section, which I-inverts into itself. The axis notes also fill in the analytic scheme between I(H) and the next H-form coming up. (We are not invoking h-forms in this context. We cannot obtain h-forms by applying T or I operations to H-forms.)

In sum, example 3.3 shows an H-structure moving from H to I(H) via transformation I; the music then states the axis pitch classes of that transformation. Next, the H-structure moves from I(H) to T9(H) via transformation J. Just as before, the music concludes the move by stating the axis pitch classes of J. These are the two dyads {E♭,D} and {A,G♯} that appear on the example with square open noteheads. J is inversion-about-E♭-and-D, or inversion-about-A-and-G♯; that is what we have just performed to get from I(H) to T9(H).

Next the H-structure moves from T9(H) to L(H) via transformation K. K is inversion-about-G-and-F♯, or inversion-about-C-and-D♭. The diamond-shaped open noteheads show how the axis dyads of K are projected by the music immediately after the axis dyads of J; K is what we are about to perform, to map T9(H) into L(H). The axis dyads of K precede, rather than follow, the effect of K in the music; that is interesting since, as we shall see later, there is a certain "retrograde" character about the final melodic gesture A♭–B♭–E–D–E♭.

Example 3.3 illustrates a transformational scheme of H-forms and axis notes-dyads that references almost every note in the piece. Only the {E,F} dyad immediately preceding L(H) is omitted from the scheme. That is a flaw, but it does not seriously undermine the cogency of the scheme.[2]

The transformational idea would be much less plausible without the form I(H) in the picture. Transformations I (from H to I(H)) and J (from I(H) to T9(H)) would also vanish. K (from T9(H) to L(H)) would still remain, but there would be too many holes in the picture: Between H and T9(H), the notes G, E♭, and E would not be members of any H-forms, nor would they have any transformational signifi-

---

2. The {E,F} dyad was also a problem on example 3.2, in connection with asserting L(h) there. The {E,F} dyad is a more serious problem in that it is hard to hear — pianissimo in a low register of the celesta, in the middle of a fairly colorful texture.

cance (for example, as axis tones). The G♯ in the middle of the piece would present the same problems.

The influence of J is particularly audible in the pitch realm, during the music surrounding its axis dyads. Example 3.5 shows how the sounding pitches of this segment arrange themselves symmetrically in registral space, and in time, about the axis dyads {E♭4,D5} and {G♯4,A4}. The upper bracket on the example groups the sustaining/repeating B♭/A with the last two notes E♭–D of the trumpet solo; the lower bracket groups that E♭–D with the following trombone solo on G♯–G. The pitches of the upper bracket serially retrograde-invert into those of the lower bracket; the pitch center is the J-axis dyad A–G♯; the temporal center is the other J-axis dyad E♭–D.[3]

Example 3.6 essentially collates various H and h forms from the piece. M is inversion about A, or about E♭. To some extent the forms of the hexachord H are represented by forms of the pentachord X = {0,1,2,5,6}, and forms of the hexachord h are represented by forms of the pentachord y = {3,4,9,10,11}. X is in Forte-class 5–6; y is in Forte-class 5–7. On example 3.6, the notes of each X-form are beamed together, and the non-X note of each H-form is flagged separately; the same obtains for y-forms and non-y notes of h-forms. On the example, in every case but one, the non-X or non-y note appears at the beginning or at the end of the hexachord presentation, so that

Example 3.5. The retro-
grade J-inversion of
pitches near the center of
Op. 10, No. 4.

3. The retrograde inversion also illustrates the transformation RICH (Lewin 1987, 180).

Example 3.6. Forms of X, H, y, h, and their (pseudo-) aggregates, listed "in order of appearance."

the beamed pentachord is temporally connected within itself. (The Ab at the "end of H" on the example, attacked in the music together with the accompanying trichord below, is the last note of the Hauptstimme to sound within the musical presentation of H.)

Abstractly, the following relations obtain. Given any form of H (resp. h), there is a unique form of X (resp. y) included within it. Given any form of X (resp. y), there is a unique form of H (resp. h) that includes it.[4] In this sense, forms of X and y can be asserted as synechdochical for the corresponding forms of H and h.

Example 3.6 uses the synechdoche to assert pseudo-aggregates

4. The two sentences do not say the same thing. Given a major third, there is a unique augmented triad that includes it. Given an augmented triad, there is not a unique major third that it includes.

74

involving "H and h" forms. Thus I(y) stands for I(h), and I(H) is thereby embedded in a "pseudo-aggregate of I-forms." The D♭ that would be necessary to extend I(y) to I(h) is indicated on the example by a crossed-out D♭ notehead. Similarly, M(X) stands for M(H), and M(h) is thereby embedded in a pseudo-aggregate of M-forms. The B♭ that would be necessary to extend M(X) to M(H) is indicated on the example by a crossed-out B♭ notehead. Finally L(y) can stand for L(h); thus we do not need to assert all of L(h) in order to embed L(H) in a pseudo-aggregate of L-forms. The A that extends L(y) to L(h) is inflected on the example by a question mark. This is exactly where we previously found it awkward to hop over G♯; the synechdoche means that we need not do so, if we are willing to accept L(y) here rather than all of L(h).

Using the synechdoche as necessary, all the H- and h-forms of example 3.6 can be embedded in appropriate (pseudo-) aggregates, with one exception. T2(H) does not extend convincingly; it seems farfetched to assert any T2(h), or even T2(y). In the context, however, T2(H) can be asserted as a synechdochical "deficient aggregate," allowing it to enter into transformational relations with other set forms and (pseudo-) aggregates. Example 3.6 lists the (pseudo-) aggregates in the order they are projected by the music.

Example 3.7 modifies example 3.4. The basic transformational progression I,J,K leads not simply from H through I(H) and T9(H) to L(H), but more generally from "T0-things" through "I-things" and "T9-things" to "L-things." By an "I-thing" one means any and all of the objects I(X), I(H), I(y), I(h), and the (pseudo-) aggregate formed by I-hexachords, as these objects interrelate in various ways. The J-arrow on example 3.7 means that if one starts with some I-thing and applies the transformation J (inverting the given I-thing about {D,E♭}

$$T0 \xrightarrow{\ I\ } I \xrightarrow{\ J\ } T9 \xrightarrow{\ K\ } L$$
things things things things

Example 3.7. The basic transformational progression.

75

or {G#,A}), one obtains the corresponding T9-thing — whether pentachord, hexachord, or (pseudo-) aggregate.

The tally of example 3.6 lists not only the things logged in example 3.7, but also three more sorts of things: T2-things, M-things, and T11-things. One naturally asks: can these three things be adjoined to the scheme of example 3.7 in a transformationally plausible way? The answer is yes. To begin the exercise, one notes a transformational proportion: T2-things are related to T0-things as T11-things are related to T9-things. That is, a T2-thing is T2-of-the-corresponding-T0-thing; a T11-thing is analogously T2-of-the-corresponding-T9-thing. We can now provisionally enlarge example 3.7 to example 3.8, using the vertical dimension of the page to graph T2-relations.

On example 3.6, M-things come between T2-things and T11-things (in order of musical projection). It seems logical, then, to try adjoining M-things to example 3.8, putting them "between T2-things and T11-things" in the middle of the second rank. A natural question then arises: Can we add a third vertical T2-arrow to example 3.8, extending downward from I-things to M-things? No, we cannot, but we can add a T10-arrow in that position. That is, any M-thing is T10-of-the-corresponding-I-thing. The T10-arrow is really better than a T2-arrow; since we are transposing inverted forms of things here, it makes good sense to complement the interval of transposition.

We have extended example 3.8 by putting M-things in the middle of its lower rank, and drawing a T10-arrow down from I-things to M-things. We now have a second rank on the figure, comprising T2-things, M-things, and T11-things. The plausibility of the arrangement

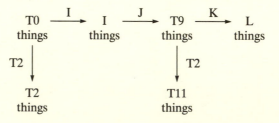

Example 3.8. The basic transformational progression elaborated by further T2-relations.

is confirmed when we investigate appropriate transformations for horizontal arrows along the second rank. Example 3.9 shows the result. To transform a T2-thing into the corresponding M-thing, one applies the transformation I (inverting about E, or about B♭); to transform an M-thing into the corresponding T11-thing, one applies the transformation J (inverting about {D,E♭}, or about {G♯,A}). Thus, on example 3.9, one sees how the basic I,J,K progression along the top rank is echoed by an I,J progression of "accessory things" along the second rank. The echo reminds one of a subplot in an Elizabethan drama.

The secondary I,J progression confirms the propriety of the T10 arrow down from I-things to M-things. As it turns out, T10 is also the transformation that converts an M-thing into the corresponding L-thing; accordingly, a T10-arrow appears on the third rank of example 3.9 pointing down from M-things to L-things. The L-things at the bottom of the example are at the end of a vertical T10,T10 progression that takes us through the various inverted things of the piece. The goal of that progression is in a different "place" (node) on the example than is the goal of the I,J,K progression along the first rank, where L-things also appear at the extreme right. One could

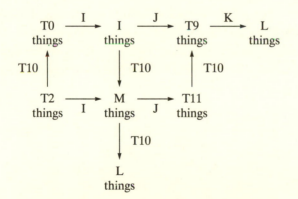

Example 3.9. The basic transformational progression elaborated by T10-relations and the I,J "subplot" along the second rank. All the things of example 3.6 are referenced.

draw a two-way arrow between the two nodes that contain L-things, labeling the arrow with transformation T0. But I do not find that necessary or even particularly desirable in this context.

On example 3.9, upward-pointing T10-arrows replace the downward-pointing T2-arrows of example 3.9. This is largely a matter of taste; one could also include both downward T2-arrows and upward T10-arrows in each case. I do not like the downward T2-arrow from T9-things to T11-things because I did not like the picture of two arrows pointing toward T11-things and no arrows pointing away from them. Given my sense of the piece, I wanted the nodes that contain L-things to be the only "output nodes" of the graph (Lewin 1987, 207).

Example 3.10 shows two trichord derivations that interact cogently with the inversion operations I and J. Derivation 1 does not reference the low F3 near the beginning of the piece. Otherwise the two derivations reference every note of the music up to the final violin solo, Ab6–Bb5–E5–D5–Eb6, which is free of the derivations. The two derivations do not overlap, except at the sustained/repeated Bb5/A4 in the middle of the piece. The trichords of derivation 1, in order to form a strict serial derivation, must be ordered by register rather than by chronology. That is logical enough, since the trichords are articulated one from another by relative tessitura as much as by chronology. Ordered registrally from the bottom up, the serial derivation is C–D–G / Db–Gb–Ab / Eb–F–Bb / E–A–B; each ordered trichord is a serial form of any other. Actually, only one aspect of the chronological ordering is incompatible with this structure: the final F of the passage

Example 3.10. Two trichord derivations.

"ought to come" between the Eb and the Bb. It does not come between them chronologically, but it does do so registrally.

The trichords of derivation 2 also form a strict serial derivation, Bb–A–Eb / D–G#–G / F#–C–Db / E–F–B. Here the trichords are articulated by chronology rather than by relative tessitura. The trichord-ordering is also chronological, except that bottom-to-top registral ordering is used when two notes are attacked more or less simultaneously, as with the trill on C–Db and the verticality E–F.

We shall not use the serial aspect of the derivations in what follows; we shall simply use the unordered trichords from the derivation-aggregates. The discussion above, anent the ordering of trichords, was only to establish that the "derivations" are in fact derivations in the rigorous serial sense of the term. Their strictness, I feel, is particularly audible in the liberating effect of the final violin solo, which breaks free from them.

Example 3.11 shows all transpositional and inversional relations among the unordered trichords of derivation 1. The trichord named at the left of each row is mapped into the trichord named at the top of each column by either of the two transformations listed in the box where each row meets each column. So, for example, the second row has {Db,Gb,Ab} at its left, and the fourth column has {E,A,B} at its top; in the box where the second row meets the fourth column appear the two transformations T3 and J. Thus, either T3 or J will map {Db,Gb,Ab} into {E,A,B}.

	{C, D, G}	{Db, Gb, Ab}	{Eb, F, Bb}	{E, A, B}
{C, D, G}	T0, T6I	T6, I	T3, J	T9, T6J
{Db, Gb, Ab}	T6, I	T0, T6I	T9, T6J	T3, J
{Eb, F, Bb}	T9, J	T3, T6J	T0, I	T6, T6I
{E, A, B}	T3, T6J	T9, J	T6, T6I	T0, I

Example 3.11. Transformational relations among the unordered trichords of derivation 1.

The structuring influence of I and J is manifest on the example. {C,D,G} and {D♭,G♭,A♭} are mapped each into the other via I. We already observed this in discussing the audibility of I at the opening of the piece; the pitches of the two trichords actually I-invert in register there, about B♭4 as a center. Inspecting example 3.11 further, we observe that {E♭,F,B♭} I-inverts into itself, as does {E,A,B}. The transformation I thus engages all four trichords of the derivation. So does the transformation J, which, as the example shows us, maps {C,D,G} and {E♭,F,B♭} each into the other while also mapping {D♭,G♭,A♭} and {E,A,B} each into the other.

Because of the way the trichords are laid out in register, the T3-relation between {C,D,G} and {E♭,F,B♭} is more easily audible in the music than is the J-relation. Likewise, the T3-relation between {D♭,G♭,A♭} and {E,A,B} is more easily audible in the music than is the J-relation. Nevertheless, the abstract J-relations between trichords are significant. In just this region of the piece, I(H) is being J-mapped into T9(H), projecting part of our I,J,K story. A useful notion is that of T3 and J as "contextual synonyms," given the trichordal system. In transforming earlier trichords to later trichords, we cannot distinguish between the effect of T3 and J on the unordered sets of pitch classes. The (registral layout of the) music makes T3 easier to hear than J, so far as the pitches in register are concerned. But T3 and J are contextually synonymous in the forward-progressing trichordal system, so far as pitch-class transformation of the unordered trichords is concerned.

Example 3.12 lays out a transformation-table for the unordered trichords of derivation 2. Again one notes the structuring influence of I and J. The influence of J is particularly audible in the music when {B♭,A,E♭} progresses to {D,G♯,G}. That was discussed earlier in connection with example 3.5, which showed a retrograde-J-inversional layout of pitches in register engaging the two temporally-ordered trichords.

The two derivations can be related via all-combinatorial hexachords of Forte-type 6–7. Example 3.13 shows the first two trichords of derivation 1 collected to form the hexachord Q of that type. The second two trichords of derivation 1 are subsumed into Q', the com-

	{B♭, A, E♭}	{D, G♯, G}	{F♯, C, D♭}	{E, F, B}
{B♭, A, E♭}	T0	J	T3	T6I
{D, G♯, G}	J	T0	I	T9
{F♯, C, D♭}	T9	I	T0	J
{E, F, B}	T6I	T3	J	T0

Example 3.12. Transformational relations among the unordered trichords of derivation 2.

Example 3.13. Hexachords of Forte-type 6–7.

plement of Q. Q′ also subsumes the first trichord of derivation 2. The second and third trichords of derivation 2 are collected to form Qbis, reprising Q as a collection of pitch classes. The final trichord of derivation 2, {E,F,B}, is left out of the Q game. In this context, the quasi Q-ness of the final violin solo is very audible. The example beams the pentachord and suggests that it might be analyzed as a defective Q-form; the missing pitch class would be A. The suggestion is stimulating, though the analysis will not be maintained in just that form. We shall return to the matter very shortly.

Transformational relations involving Q (or Qbis) and Q′ are displayed on example 3.14. Q maps into itself via inversion I; so does Q′. Q and Q′ map, each into the other, via inversion J. T3 is again a contextual synonym for J. T3 is the most audible transformation of Q to Q′ in the music because of the way the pitches are laid out in register.

Let us return now to the idea suggested by the end of example 3.13, that the violin solo might be a defective Q-form lacking the

	Q	Q'
Q	T0, T6, I, T6I	T3, T9, J, T6J
Q'	T3, T9, J, T6J	T0, T6, I, T6I

Example 3.14. Transformational relations involving Q and Q'.

Example 3.15. P-pentachords (of Forte-type 5–15).

pitch class A. There are problems that make it difficult to maintain the idea. First, unlike Q, Q', and Qbis of example 3.13, the violin solo does not engage any trichordal derivation of the music. On the contrary, the violin passage sounds notably liberated from the derivations of example 3.10, as we observed earlier. Then, too, one finds it hard to imagine a hypothetical pitch class A that combines with the violin solo to project a Q-form, when there is in fact a sustained (repeated) B in the music that combines with the solo to project an H-form. Indeed, from a completely abstract point of view, the pentachord of the violin solo (5–15) is as good a synechdoche for H as it is for Q. H includes only one form of 5–15, whereas Q includes two distinct forms of the pentachord. (H does not give a strictly better synechdoche than Q; a given form of 5–15 extends to only one form of Q, but it extends to two distinct forms of H.)

These considerations suggest that we study the 5–15 forms of the piece in their own right, as pivotal pentachords that can engage both H and Q forms. Example 3.15 displays the most audible forms of 5–15 as presented in the music, labeling them as the "first" through the "last" forms to appear, respectively. The first form, comprising C, D, D♭, G♭, and A♭, is also labeled "P"; this form is embedded in the hexachord earlier labeled "H," and also in the hexachord earlier labeled "Q." The pentachords are labeled "first" through "last," rather than "P", "I(P)", and so forth, because the transformational labels are not abstractly univocal. The second form, for example, which can logically be labeled "I(P)," might abstractly be labeled "T6(P)" because of the pentachord's intrinsic symmetry. In any case, we are less interested in transformational labels for the individual P-forms than we are in exploring specific transformations that carry us from each form to the next in the composition.

Example 3.16 graphs the most audible such transformations. The second form is easily heard as the I-inversion of the first, because the pitches of the first form (as on example 3.15) invert in register about B♭4 into the pitches of the second form. The third form can easily be heard as the T3-transpose of the second, because the pitch classes of the third form, as temporally presented on example 3.15, T3-retrograde the pitch classes of the second form, as temporally presented. Indeed, the temporally ordered pitches of the third form, in register, are the exact retrograde of the second form three semitones higher, except for the opening pitch C5 of the second form and the (corresponding) closing pitch E♭4 of the third form. The last P-form can easily be heard as the T5-transpose of the third, because the pitch classes of the last form, as temporally presented on example 3.15, T5-retrograde the pitch classes of the third form, as temporally presented. Indeed, the temporally ordered pitches of the last form, in register, are the exact retrograde of the third form five semitones higher, except for the closing pitch E♭4 of the third form, and the (corresponding) opening pitch A♭6 of the last form.

Example 3.17 supplements the analysis of the preceding paragraph by displaying some tetrachordal subsets of the P-forms that belong to Forte-class 4–5. The relative registral positioning of the pitches within each tetrachord is preserved by I, T3, and T5 in turn. The

$$\text{first} \xrightarrow{\text{I}} \text{second} \xrightarrow{\text{(R)T3}} \text{third} \xrightarrow{\text{(R)T5}} \text{last}$$

Example 3.16. The most audible transformational progressions of the P-forms.

Example 3.17. Registrally inverted and transposed 4–5 tetrachords within the P-forms, also temporarily retrograded.

	first	second	third	last
first	T0, T6I	T6, I	T9, T6J	T2, L
second	T6, I	T0, T6I	T3, J	T8, T6L
third	T3, T6J	T9, J	T0, I	T5, K
last	T10, L	T4, T6L	T7, K	T0, M

Example 3.18. Transformational relations among the unordered P-forms.

transformations are easy to hear when the tetrachords are gathered into verticalities, as on the left side of the example. Then one can quickly pick up the retrograde-transpositional relationships among the ordered tetrachords displayed on the right side of the example. After listening to example 3.17 for a while, the reader can go back to example 3.15, where the retrograde-T3–relation between the second and third P-forms will now be easier to hear, as will the retrograde-T5–relation between the third and the last P-forms.

Example 3.16 tells an aurally convincing story. We can call it "the I,T3,T5 story." But what has happened to our earlier "I,J,K story," which was so intellectually convincing in a number of ways? Can the two stories coexist?

Example 3.18 begins to explore that question by listing all the abstract transformational relationships among the P-forms of example 3.15, considered now as unordered sets of pitch classes. On this table of relationships, J is contextually synonymous with T3; the third P-form of pitch classes is abstractly the J-inversion of the second form, as well as its T3-transpose. Likewise, K is contextually synonymous with T5; the last P-form is abstractly the K-inversion of the third form, as well as its T5-transpose. From this point of view, one could say that the "I,T3,T5 story" of P-forms is contextually synonymous for an "I,J,K story" of those forms.

Example 3.19 fleshes out the idea. Beneath the notes of the example, brackets group H, I(H), T9(H), and L(H), the four H-forms that project the basic I,J,K progression of H-forms. The I,J,K progression is depicted by downward-looping arrows connecting one H-form to the next, reproducing an earlier picture (example 3.4). Within each H-form, the notes of the corresponding P-form discussed above are beamed together, and the note of the H-form that does not belong to the P-form is flagged separately. The flagged notes are all either registral or temporal boundaries: the flagged F3 is the lowest pitch in the presentation of its hexachord, and it occurs at the end of that presentation; the flagged E♭5 and D5 are the final notes of their respective hexachord presentations; the flagged B4 is the first and lowest note of its hexachord presentation.

At the top of example 3.19, upward-arching arrows depict the I,T3,T5 progression of P-forms explored in the discussion of examples 3.15–17. The T3-arrow is labeled "T3(or J)," because J is a contextual synonym for T3 in the context. Likewise, the T5-arrow is labeled "T5(or K)" and — to be consistent — the I-arrow is labeled "I(or T6)." The example illustrates how the I,T3,T5 progression of

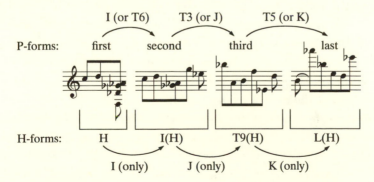

Example 3.19. The P-forms in their embedding H-forms.

P-forms coexists with the I,J,K progression of H-forms. The I,T3,T5 progression is the easiest chain of transformations to hear in moving from one P-form to the next. Yet it would not be false to describe the progression of P-forms as a (contextually synonymous) I,J,K progression. And when the P-forms are quasi-synechdochically embedded in their surrounding H-forms, the cogency of the I,J,K progression becomes something more than "not false." Although the I,T3,T5 chain does not extend to the embedding hexachords, the I,J,K chain does.

Example 3.19 sheds some light on how the I,T3,T5 story can coexist with the I,J,K story. But the example, in doing so, seems to portray a paradox. If the idea is to show that the progression of P-forms is consistent with the progression of H-forms, why did not Webern lay out the pitches and temporal orderings of the P-forms so as to emphasize the J- and K-relations among them, rather than the T3 and T5 relations? Should one conclude that the I,J,K progression of H-forms — as shown in examples 3.3–5 and 3.7–9 — is an intellectual chimera without musical significance?

I do not think so. I sense the matter somewhat as follows. The pc structures we have been studying fall into two general categories, "symmetrical" structures and "asymmetrical" ones. The symmetrical structures are the trichordal derivations and the Q-forms; the asymmetrical structures are the H-forms, together with their synechdochical X/y pentachords and their pseudo-aggregates. To some extent, the P-forms belong in both symmetrical and asymmetrical camps. Abstractly, each P-form is a symmetrical pc structure: it inverts into itself. The abstract symmetry allows for the possibility of contextual synonyms, like those of example 3.18, when one is transforming P-forms one into another. P-forms can be heard as quasi-synechdochical for symmetrical Q-forms in certain analytic contexts, too, as with the violin solo at the end of example 3.13.

On the other hand, P-forms are more often — and more unequivocally — heard in the context of the H-forms that embed them in the music; this is the idea of example 3.19. Here each H-form fixes its embedded abstractly symmetrical P-form into either an unambiguously "prime" or unambiguously "inverted" ambience. The unambiguously determined asymmetyrical H-forms progress through the I,J,K story, and the P-forms-as-H-subsets must perforce follow that progression. The point of the I,T3,T5 story is to demonstrate the symmetry of the P-forms-in-themselves, notwithstanding the asymmetrical H-context. The P-forms have the potential to liberate themselves from asymmetrical H-contexts, to display their intrinsic symmetries, and to align themselves with other symmetric configurations in the music.

A paradigmatic sonorous image for the idea just discussed is provided by the opening sonority from the previous movement of the same work. The first twenty-five seconds or so of Webern's Op. 10, No. 3 are sketched in example 3.20. In the example, the opening sonority of the piece is marked with a symbolic tremolo sign and labeled "Shimmer." This sonority is produced by mandolin (tremolo in thirty-second notes), guitar (likewise), celesta (repeated quarters), and harp (repeated eighths). A deep orchestral bell and cowbells color the sonority for about the first twenty-one seconds; then a rolling bass drum takes over from the orchestral bell, darkening the sound.

The lowest five pitches of the Shimmer sonority project the P-form {G♯3,E4,A4,D5,B♭5}. This P-form, which is abstractly symmetrical about the pitch class A, is laid out in register so that its pitches are pitch-inversionally symmetrical about the pitch center A4. The top note of the Shimmer sonority, C♯6, embeds the P-form in an H-form (specifically T8(H), if we continue reckoning "H" to be the first six notes of Op. 10, No. 4). Given the inversional symmetry of the Shimmering P-pitches, the high C♯ maximally discombobulates the symmetric structure, emphasizing the asymmetry of the H-form. The layout of the pitches is indeed paradigmatic, demonstrating "the sym-

Shimmer   Tune   Shimmer'

Example 3.20. Some aspects of Webern, Orchestral Piece, Op. 10, No. 3.

metry of the P-forms-in-themselves, notwithstanding the asymmetrical H-context." The P-forms, as observed above, "have the potential to liberate themselves from asymmetrical H-contexts, to display their intrinsic symmetries, and to align themselves with other symmetric configurations in the music."

Another such symmetric configuration is the figure marked "Tune" on example 3.20, that is, the melody F5–B3–F♯4–C5, presented by the violin. The pitches of the Tune do not align themselves symmetrically about a pitch center, but the pitch classes of the Tune are very symmetrical. The Tune is its own retrograde J-inversion, as a succession of pitch classes; the Tune as an unordered pcset is also its own T6-transpose and its own T6J-inversion.

Since the pitch structure of the Shimmer sonority is almost symmetrical by inversion about A4, there is a certain urge for the high C♯6 of the Shimmer to be "answered" by a low F3. That does not happen in example 3.20, but we can hear in the example that the next pitch class, after (about six seconds of) Shimmer, is an F, specifically the F5 that begins the Tune. The C♯ is thus answered as a pitch class, if not as a pitch. The pitch F3 does not appear in Op. 10, No. 3, but it does appear very audibly as the first "bass note" of Op. 10, No. 4, where it is coupled into a verticality beneath D♭4. Perhaps the low {F3,D♭4} dyad at the opening of Op. 10, No. 4 answers by inversion-about-A4 the high C♯6 of Shimmer plus the F5 of the Tune.

That is quite conjectural. Much clearer is the desire of the Shimmer C♯ to find some F that answers it by pitch-class inversion-about-A. The F at the beginning of the Tune is one such F. An even stronger F appears at the reprise of the Shimmer sonority. This passage, sketched on example 3.20 by the symbols labeled "Shimmer'," starts with the return of C♯6 in m. 7, sounding by itself in the mandolin (tremolo in thirty-seconds) over the orchestral bell. After about three seconds of this sonority, other instruments join the mandolin and bell: harmonium repeating its note in triplet eights, celesta playing a slow trill in eighths, harp repeating a harmonic in quarters, a sustained cello harmonic, and cowbells. Shimmer' "answers" its initial C♯6 by F6 and fills in the entire chromatic cluster from C♯6 to F6 inclusive; no other pitches are notated for the non-bell instruments.

Pitch-class inversion about A (or about E♭) is again strongly projected, now by the symmetry of the cluster. Also projected again is the desire of an initially "asymmetrical" C♯ to be answered by some "balancing" F. The Shimmer' sonority is prolonged for about thirty seconds, through a new Tune', up to the point where the instruments of definite pitch disappear from the piece. Among other things, this increases our ability to connect aurally the {C♯,F} dyads of Op. 10, No. 3 with the low {F3,D♭4} dyad in the first chord of Op. 10, No. 4.

Earlier, we used the letter M to denote pitch-class inversion about A (or about E♭). Using that terminology now, we can say that Shimmer' reprises not only textural aspects of Shimmer but also the structural idea of M-symmetry, as well as the urge for C♯ to find its M-partner F. We can say in particular that the P-form within Shimmer is "M-symmetrical," meaning that it M-inverts into itself. The M-symmetry of Shimmer' then projects, inter alia, the potential of the P-forms "to liberate themselves from asymmetrical H-contexts, to display their intrinsic symmetries, and to align themselves with other symmetric configurations in the music."

This last observation can help us hear another connection between Op. 10, No. 3 and Op. 10, No. 4 — specifically, between the Shimmer P-form at the beginning of No. 3, which is M-symmetrical, and the last P-form (violin solo) of No. 4, which is also M-symmetrical. Example 3.21 helps us focus on the connection, and puts it in a larger

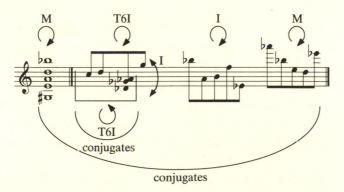

Example 3.21. Some symmetries involving P-forms of Webern, Op. 10, Nos. 3 and 4.

context. The Shimmer P-form and the violin solo at the end of Op. 10, No. 4 are labeled "conjugates" on example 3.21; the first and second P-forms of Op. 10, No. 4 are also labeled conjugates. One sees and hears what this term means: Two different P-forms are "conjugates" of each other if each is symmetrical under the same inversion operation, or if they jointly add up to a Q-form, or if they are T6-transposes of each other, or if they share the same {0,2,6,8}-type (4–25) tetrachord — all these conditions for "conjugacy" being formally equivalent so far as P-forms are concerned.

Using example 3.21, one can hear something corresponding to the "conjugate" idea without much difficulty as one listens to the Shimmer P-form and the violin solo of Op. 10, No. 4 in this context. The violin solo, marked "wie ein Hauch," seems inter alia to make a quasi-echo for the Shimmer sonority. Or perhaps the idea of reincarnation, rather than echo, provides a better metaphor for the aural effect of the conjugate relationship. The conjugacy of the first and second P-forms, heard at the opening of Op. 10, No. 4, also seems significant for the compositional effect; at the end of Op. 10, No. 4 one hears that the conjugate relation of violin solo to Shimmer P-form is the same as the previously heard conjugate relation of second P-form to first. The proportion involves the opening of Op. 10, No. 3; the opening of No. 4; and the end of No. 4. This helps one pick up the proportion aurally.

Example 3.21 references all four (aurally prominent) P-forms of Op. 10, No. 4, as well as the single (aurally prominent) P-form of Op. 10, No. 3. The P-forms of Op. 10, No. 4 are being explored here for their internal symmetries rather than for the transformations that carry each form to the next. In a terminology I have developed elsewhere (Lewin 1987, 142), the transformations labeling the arrows of example 3.21 are (for the most part) "internal" for the P-forms, unlike the transformations labeling the arrows of example 3.19, which are "progressive" for successive P-forms — and for successive H-forms.

On example 3.21, operation M is displayed as internal for both the Shimmer P-form and its conjugate, the violin solo at the end of Op. 10, No. 4. M- symmetry, as projected by the opening and reprise of Op. 10, No. 3, has a strong tonic quality for that piece. On the example, operation I is displayed as internal for the Q-hexachord that subsumes the first two P-forms. The I-relation between those two conjugate pentachords is very audible because of the pitch symmetry about B♭4, already much discussed here; I-symmetry has a strong tonic quality at the opening of Op. 10, No. 4. A new feature of example 3.21, not previously discussed, is the internal I-symmetry of the third P-form in Op. 10, No. 4. Though the third P-form is moving away from the second, via T3 (or J) as on example 3.19, the internal symmetry of the third P-form is still prolonging the influence of I. In like manner, the fourth P-form (that is, the violin solo) of Op. 10, No. 4, although moving away from the third form via T5 (or K), is also recalling the influence of M, a transformation strongly associated with key events in Op. 10, No. 3, among them the P-form of Shimmer.[5]

The preceding remarks about Op. 10, No. 3 do not constitute an adequate study of pitch structure in the piece, even in its opening. Example 3.22 illustrates one aspect of the opening that lies beyond the boundaries of our discussion so far. The example shows how the total chromatic is laid out so as to be virtually pitch-symmetrical in register about the new pitch-center B♭4–B4. Open noteheads indicate

Example 3.22. Symmetrical spacing of the total chromatic about the pitch-center B♭4–B4, at the opening of Webern, Op. 10, No. 3.

5. The violin solo of Op. 10, No. 4 also associates aurally with the M-symmetrical Shimmer' cluster. The high notes of the violin solo, A♭6, B♭5, and E♭6, recall the register of Shimmer' and the role of E♭6 specifically as center of a pitch-inversion. E♭6 is the last note of the violin solo, and of Op. 10, No. 4; the relation to Shimmer', once noticed, is not hard to focus upon aurally.

pitches of the Shimmer hexachord; solid noteheads without stems indicate pitches of the Tune. A solid notehead with a stem indicates E♭5, the first note heard after Shimmer and the Tune (m. 3, horn). The next event in the piece (m. 4) is a vertical simultaneity containing G3, the twelfth pitch class of the piece; example 3.22 indicates G4 (which is where the pitch class G belongs in the registral scheme) by another solid notehead with a stem. The upper six notes of the example project an all-combinatorial hexachord of Forte-class 6–8; the lower six notes project the complementary hexachord of the same class.

The cautionary note struck by example 3.22 should not be taken so strongly as to call into question the analytic work accomplished so far. Example 3.23, sketching the pitches of Op. 10, No. 1, shows how forms of h, y, H, X, and P exercise a lively structuring influence on this music. All pitches are included except those that accompany the first melodic gesture on the upper staff of the example, which is a strong Hauptstimme. The opening B–C of the piece recurs an octave lower to lead off the bass of the accompaniment, with D–E♭ above (mm. 4–5); we lack space to expand on this aspect of the analysis

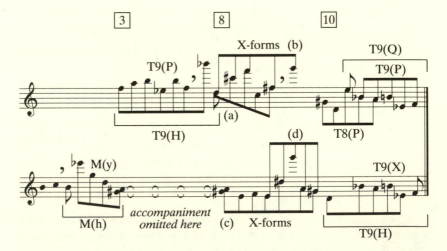

Example 3.23. Pitches of Webern, Orchestral Piece, Op. 10, No. 1, indicating some audible forms of X, y, H, h, P, and Q.

here. The pcset M(y) recurs as a simultaneity of the accompaniment (including G#–A), where it supports the second high B of the Hauptstimme; M(y) and the high B together project M(h), which thus also recurs here as a simultaneity.

The reader is encouraged to check the groupings of example 3.23 against the full score. The example articulates the piece into four sections. The first comprises the opening B–C and a statement of M(h); the section cadences into the long trill on G# and A. The second section occurs while the trill is being prolonged. A prominent melodic Hauptstimme in the upper register projects T9(P), extending to T9(H). Since T9(P) is symmetrical, it could also be labeled as an "inverted" P-form; the transpositional label is chosen here simply to conform with the label for the embedding H-form. Indeed, this P-form is the "third P-form" of Op. 10, No. 4; the reader can find it on example 3.21. The P-form, as one sees there, is I-symmetrical. T9(H) itself is a "basic H-form" of Op. 10, No. 4; one finds it displayed as such on example 3.1.

A third section of Op. 10, No. 1, on example 3.23, is articulated by the end of the long trill, a complicated network of X-forms, and an eventual return to the dyad A4–G#4, though no longer as a trill. The X-forms are labeled (a), (b), (c), and (d) on the example; as we shall not undertake a thorough transformational analysis of Op. 10, No. 1, T/I transformational labels would clutter the example to no purpose. Later we shall explore some different sorts of relationships among the X-forms of section 3.

The fourth section of example 3.23 reprises T9(P) and its embedding T9(H) (in the lower register). That gives the melodic Hauptstimme of section 2 an even greater structuring force for the composition, a force that encourages us to hear as more weighty the later recurrence of the T9(P) and T9(H) forms within Op. 10, No. 4. The T9(P) form at the end of example 3.23 is directly preceded by a form labeled T8(P). We noted above that T9(P) is I-symmetrical; now we note that T8(P) is M-symmetrical. In fact it is the same pcset as the Shimmer P-form from Op. 10, No. 3. The pitches of T8(P), like those of the Shimmer P-form, are disposed symmetrically in register about A4. In sum, the pcsets marked "T8(P)" and "T9(P)" on example 3.23

are identical, respectively, with the first pcset of example 3.21 and the I-symmetrical pcset of the same example, whereas the pcset marked "T9(H)" on example 3.23 is identical with the pcset so labeled in the middle of example 3.1.

T9(P), at the end of example 3.23, is embedded in T9(Q) as well as T9(H). The symmetric potential of the H-embedded P-form is thus highlighted by an appropriate P-embedding Q-form; the idea is familiar from Op. 10, No. 4. The final T9(H) of example 3.23 articulates T9(X) (its first five notes) as well as T9(P) (its last five notes). T9(X) provides a link between the X-forms of section 3 and the T9(H) form of section 4.

In the music, the X-form labeled (b) on example 3.23 is a clear Hauptstimme for section 3. We shall call it the "Hauptstimme X-form." Its thematic nature is reinforced by its appearance in a later Hauptstimme, the clarinet melody that initiates the middle section of Op. 10, No. 3. Example 3.24 displays the Hauptstimme X-form there. It is accompanied by a J-related form, as indicated. Quite audible is the absence of any common tone between the two X-forms. The two pentachords fill a complete decachord of the total chromatic, a decachord of Forte-type 10–1.

A bit of experimenting will convince the reader of the following fact: Given any X-form, there is one and only one other X-form that has no common tone with the given X-form. We shall call the two forms "10–1 associates"; their union is a form of that decachord. We can also define a transformation on forms of X, a transformation

Example 3.24. The Hauptstimme X-form of Op. 10, No. 3.

called ASSOC(10–1): Applying the transformation to a form of X yields the 10–1 associate of the given form.

Using this idea, we could label the lower X-form of example 3.23 as ASSOC(10–1)(Haupt X). In the case of the specific form Haupt X, applying ASSOC(10–1) yields the same result as does applying J-inversion, but ASSOC(10–1) does not have the same effect on all X-forms as does J. An additional distinction between the two transformations is that J can be performed on any pcset, or indeed on any individual pitch class; ASSOC(10–1) is defined only on forms of X as arguments. ASSOC(10–1) is a "contextual" operation on forms of X.

Transformations like J are useful when we want to interrelate the J-transformation of X-forms with the J-transformation of y-forms or H-forms or h-forms (as with the "things" of examples 3.7–9), or with J-symmetries of sets or derivations, or with axes of J-inversion in the music, and so forth. Transformations like ASSOC(10–1) are useful when we are interrelating various forms of X strictly among themselves; the 10–1 association between two X-forms is often easy to hear. For instance, one can hear it on example 3.23, where the relation obtains between the X-forms (a) and (d) of section 3. Indeed, the ten pitch classes projected by the associated X-forms (a) and (d) exhaust the pitch-class content of section 3. Pentachord (a) begins as section 3 begins, pentachord (d) begins immediately after pentachord (a) ends, and pentachord (d) ends as section 3 ends; the associated X-forms thus exhaust the temporal extent of the section as well as its pitch-class content.

In like manner, we can talk of an "ASSOC(4–7) relation" between X-forms (a) and (b) on example 3.23; the two X-forms are associated via their common tetrachord of Forte-form 4–7, here the tetrachord {D,C♯,F,F♯}. (In general, given any X-form, there will be a unique other X-form that shares the same 4–7 subset.) Similarly, we can talk of an "ASSOC(4–8) relation" between X-forms (c) and (d); the two X-forms are associated via their common tetrachord of Forte-form 4–8, here the tetrachord {D♯,E,G♯,A}. (In general, given any X-form, there will be a unique other X-form that shares the same 4–8 subset.)

One may feel a certain methodological uneasiness, interrelating X-forms by ASSOC operations here and T/I operations there. But the uneasiness can be quelled by further reflection. First, there is no general methodological rationale for asserting that a certain X-form "is" in one and only one relation to another X-form, independent of any larger context. Elsewhere (Lewin 1986, 357–73; 1987, 95–98) I have discussed such misuse of the verb "to be," especially in its present tense. There is no reason, for instance, to decide a priori that the two X-forms of example 3.24 cannot "be" 10–1 associates and also J-related "at the same time." (The semantic problem with that temporal metaphor is carefully criticized in Lewin 1986.) Leaving aside such general matters, let us turn to the specific analytic discourse at hand. Therein, the ASSOC operations have not been mixed promiscuously with the T/I operation; rather the ASSOC operations have been invoked strictly within passages of the music that focus upon X-forms fitting together. Example 3.24 shows such a passage, as does the third section of example 3.23. As we broaden our analytic focus beyond the limits of such a passage, it seems perfectly logical to invoke T or I relations that can involve X-forms in themselves or as synechdochic representatives for H-forms. Thus, on example 3.23, it does not seem inconsistent to assert an M-relation between X-form (d) at the end of section 3 and X-form T9(X) at the opening of section 4. Though T9(X) begins right after X-form (d) ends, a clear boundary is crossed between the end of section 3, which includes X-form (d), and the beginning of section 4, which includes the form T9(X). In Section 4, T9(X) is interacting with T9(H), T9(P), and so forth; the X-form is no longer simply interacting locally with other X-forms, in particular with the X-forms of section 3. The asserted M-relation is plausible here because of the M-symmetrical T8(P), which connects X-form (d) to T9(X) across the section boundary. As we observed earlier, the M-symmetrical T8(P) is the same pcset as the Shimmer P-form; we also observed that T8(P) on example 3.23 supports its abstract M-symmetry by the symmetrical disposition of its pitches in register about A4 (just like the Shimmer P-form). Thus, it is not farfetched to listen for an M-inversion relation that levers X-form (d) across the M-symmetrical fulcrum T8(P), into T9(X) across the section boundary.

CHAPTER 4

A Transformational Basis
for Form and Prolongation
in Debussy's "Feux d'artifice"

The table below gives a synoptic overview of "Feux d'artifice," useful for future reference.

introduction	mm. 1–24
theme, variations	mm. 25–46
episode 1	mm. 47–56
episode 2	mm. 57–64
first reprise	mm. 65–70
episode 3	mm. 71–78
second reprise	mm. 79–86
climactic bomb, aftermath	mm. 87–89
coda	mm. 90–98

The *Marseillaise*

When the anthem appears in the coda one first takes it to be a bit of naturalistic tone-painting: The Bastille Day display of fireworks has ended with a huge climactic bomb, and the crowd is heading home. As they go, snatches of the music are heard drifting through the air from some far-off band. One reason we take the gesture in this naturalistic way is that the anthem appears *after* the piece's enormous and almost parodistically grandiose acoustic climax, well after the music has settled into a very quiet and inert drone to begin the coda. In order to take the *Marseillaise* at face value, we would expect it to appear at an obvious musical climax, as climactic material in the manner of Schumann's *Die beiden Grenadiere*, Op. 49 (at the change to the major key), or at least of his *Faschingsschwank aus Wien*, Op. 26 (no. 1 at the four-flat signature, m. 292).

Yet Debussy means the quotation very much in earnest, and its compositional placement is absolutely correct. For one thing, the quotation involves a signature, not just for this piece but for the entire collection of twenty-four preludes. The signature is "CD, musicien français." The initials C and D are represented by notes within the *Marseillaise* fragments; the title "musicien français" is represented by the anthem itself, in this respect somewhat like a little French flag marking the corner of a bustling crowd scene by Renoir.

The signature conceals a passionate nationalistic subtext after all. These are the twenty-four preludes not of J. S. Bach but of a determinedly "French" composer. Already in 1910, Debussy writes: "There's too much German influence in France and we're still suffocated by it. Don't you go the same way, don't let yourselves be taken in by false profundity and the detestable German 'modernstyl'" (Lesure and Nichols 1987, 233). Debussy's words here appear to respond in kind to Hans Sachs, at the end of *Die Meistersinger:*

Habt Acht! Uns dräuen üble Streich':
zerfällt erst deutsches Volk und Reich,
in falscher wälscher Majestät
kein Fürst bald mehr sein Volk versteht,
und wälschen Dunst mit wälschem Tand
sie pflanzen uns in deutsches Land;
was deutsch und echt, wüsst' keiner mehr, . . .

(Watch out! Evil blows threaten us. If once the German folk and land should disintegrate in spurious foreign pomp, then soon no prince would understand his people any more, foreign humbug and vanity would take root on German soil, nobody would know any more what was German and true. . . .)

In this regard, Debussy's citation from the *Marseillaise* is more than a signature; it is a call to arms. One notes that we do not hear the music for "Allons enfants de la patrie . . . "; rather we hear the explicit call to arms: "Aux armes, citoyens! Formez vos bataillons! Marchons! Marchons!"[1] The nation was to be at war not much more than a year after the piece was composed.[2] Omens of armed struggle are not hard to hear in the work. Indeed, fireworks are by their very nature a parody of bombardment. *En blanc et noir* is foreshadowed by the black-note-versus-white-note contrasts here. Images of darkness and light are also naturalistically pertinent to the fireworks display.

Example 4.1 shows how black-note/white-note contrasts are laid out from the climax to the end of the piece. "Black-note" material is labeled "B"; "white-note" material is labeled "W". At the climax

1. One hears only two musical phrases; the first phrase stands for both "Aux armes, citoyens!" and "Formez vos bataillons!" In a possible naturalistic reading, one hears "Aux armes, citoyens!"; then the next phrase is drowned out; then one hears "Marchons, marchons . . ." This reading takes place in clock time. In another possible naturalistic reading, one hears "Formez vos bataillons!"; one then takes a subjective beat, passing out of the Newtonian time-flow, to meditate on the significance of the quotation, this meditation being represented by the subjective echo of the Kopfmotiv from the main theme. Then one returns into clock time with the next line of text, "Marchons, marchons . . ."

2. ". . . a fleeting reference to the *Marseillaise* as the . . . revellers finally disperse and disappear . . . But where do these revellers disappear?" (Lockspeiser 1972, 158). Lockspeiser captures the essence of the matter beautifully here. Unfortunately, he then drifts off into a hyper-aesthetic answer involving "the illusion of an illusion, the dream of a dream, the . . . almost unheard notes of the music of silence." This will not do. Lockspeiser knew well enough where they disappeared — at least the able-bodied males. Why should one suppose Debussy less sensitive to the onrushing crisis than his contemporaries among the Central Powers? And why treat him as some sort of neurasthenic Bunthorne?

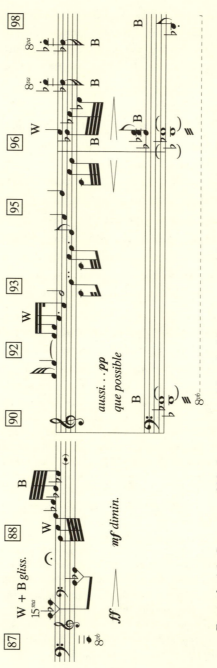

Example 4.1. Contrasts of black-note material and white-note material at the end of Debussy, "Feux d'artifice."

(m. 87), black and white note glissandos tumble downwards locked together, each one alternately higher and lower as the rhythmic 7-against-5 patterns work themselves out. The effect tone-paints ripplings of light streaming from the bomb; in the political reading, one imagines Holmes and Moriarty toppling over the cliff locked in mortal embrace. Dynamics save the climax from caricature; the cliché would be *sempre ff* or even *ff crescendo,* rather than *diminuendo* to *mf.* The diminuendo points our attention toward the (acoustic) "anticlimax" of m. 90, and thence toward the *Marseillaise.*

We hear many vertical semitone relations during the double glissando of m. 87. Because the glissandos intermesh, each alternately higher and lower, we cannot say that either interval-one relations or interval-eleven relations apply consistently from either white to black, or from black to white. The case is quite different at m. 88, which recalls m. 1–16. Here the entire white-note group F–G–A both precedes and lies lower than the entire black-note group Bb–Ab–Gb. We can certainly assert a T1-relation from the unordered white-note trichord to the unordered black-note trichord, a T1 that works both forward temporally and upwards registrally.

During m. 90–95, the situation is just as unequivocal: the black-note music involving Db and its fifth both precedes and lies below the white-note music involving C and its fifth (the *Marseillaise* plus the Kopfmotiv of the theme). We can definitely assert a T11-relation here from black to white, a T11 that works both forward temporally and upward registrally. The T11 renders the *Marseillaise* "out of tune," a phenomenon that supports both the naturalistic effect and the nationalistic anxiety. (The band is far away and we/they are departing as the crowd is babbling; "uns dräuen üble Streich'.")

From m. 96 on, after the final E5 of the *Marseillaise,* all notes are black; night enfolds everything. Even the "sparks" of mm. 96–97 are final puffs of darkness, unlike the scintillating white-note sparks of mm. 8 and 10 from which they derive, sparks that gave us signature CD dyads in the same register. The last note of the piece (m. 98) is staccato, not morendo. We are brought up abruptly, jolted as we realize that the light is gone along with the *Marseillaise.*

The T11-relation between "Db music" and "C music" during

mm. 90–95 condenses and comments upon a larger-scale Db/C relation. The first reprise (mm. 65–70) gives us a form of the theme "in C♯," whereas the second reprise (mm. 79–86) gives us the theme "in C," at its original pitch-class level. The temporal aspect of that C♯/C relation returns, condensed, in the Db/C relation of mm. 90–95. Indeed, one can hear the second reprise being prolonged into the C-major music of m. 92–95, including the *Marseillaise*. Example 4.2 shows how.

Beneath the beginning of example 4.2, a bracket at m. 82–83 indicates the Kopfmotiv of the theme from the second reprise; beneath the end of the example, another bracket at m. 93 indicates the return of the motive under the *Marseillaise*. The example as a whole shows how the two bracketed segments are bound together by a continuous process. The thematic cell from m. 83, C4–A4–G4, begins to rise chromatically over m. 84 (along with its familiar order-permutation Bb–Ab–Db, and so forth). The dynamic level rises as well. The chain of T1-relations is almost too mechanical.[3]

Over mm. 85–86, the chromatically rising thematic cell continues to develop with heavier textural and rhythmic emphasis than in the previous measures and at a yet higher dynamic level. The melodic focus shifts an octave higher, to register C6–Bb5–Eb5 and higher (doubled at yet another octave above). Wondering where the chromatic ascent will reach its goal, we are abruptly interrupted by the explosion of the climactic bomb and its aftermath; this material (mm. 87–91) is all descending in register. The "interruption" (in the present reading) is represented by large parentheses on the staff of example 4.2. At m. 92, the citation from the *Marseillaise* enters; the example shows how the opening phrase of the citation ("Aux armes, citoyens!") picks up and continues the thematic cell, raising it yet one semitone "higher" than it was at the end of m. 86. The incipit G5 of the tune is still in the upper register of mm 85–86; the E5 and D5 that complete the cell G–E–D return to the lower register of m. 84. As soon as G–E–D is complete (m. 93), the entire Kopfmotiv to the

---

3. We have discussed the almost too parodistic machinery of the climax before, and we shall do so again.

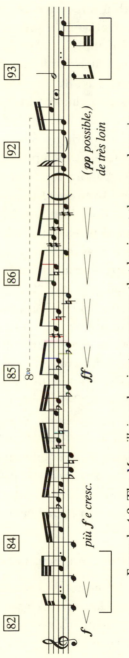

Example 4.2. The *Marseillaise* culuminates a process that begins at the second reprise.

theme returns underneath it, bracketed below on example 4.2. The brackets on the example mark out a sort of chromatic Zug that is bounded by the C–A–G of m. 83 and the G–E–D of mm. 92–93. Over this Zug, the chromatic line fills in the thematic interval C-to-G from the "horn call" figure of m. 82.

And so the *Marseillaise* is a climax after all; it is specifically the climactic goal of the process sketched in example 4.2. The analysis is difficult to grasp in a naive hearing for several reasons. One is the dynamic profile of the example, which puts at m. 92 an "anti-climactic" *pp possible, de très loin.* A more formidable reason is the acoustic climax of m. 87, subsiding over some time into a weighty cadence and an apparent structural downbeat for the entire piece "in D♭" at m. 90; this must be analyzed by example 4.2 as "interrupting" a "C-major" process that leaves off at m. 86 and resumes at m. 92.

Edward T. Cone's idea of "stratification" is suggestive here: The music of example 4.2 belongs to one "C-major" stratum; the music of mm. 87–91 belong to another "D♭" stratum (Cone 1962; the concept of stratification, illustrated by the entire essay, is formally introduced on p. 19.). However, the notion carries us only a certain distance. The essential and difficult analytic-critical task at hand is not to articulate the two strata but to integrate them. The piece contains not only the climactic C-major *Marseillaise* of example 4.2, and not only the D♭ structural downbeat of m. 90 as prepared by the climactic bomb of mm. 87ff. but also a crucial sort of metastable equilibrium between the two — an equilibrium that involves T1/T11 relationships as well as matters *en blanc et noir* (fireworks and night, light and darkness, the powers of light and the powers of darkness). We shall return to these issues for further commentary.

Introduction (mm. 1–24)

The opening introduces the total chromatic, whose twelfth note arrives with the registrally climactic E7 of m. 25. Repetitive rising-and-falling figures become motivic over the introduction, leading to that E7. Once E7 is introduced, such gestures become less immediately figural, receding into an accompanimental background; their periods and amplitudes broaden considerably. The introduction presents and/or suggests some pregnant source sets: whole-tone, chromatic, pentatonic, and diatonic. A number of these display the white-note/black-note dichotomy as they are presented. The section also introduces a number of referential transformational motifs. We have already noted the T1-relation between the unordered white-note trichord {F,G,A} of m. 1 and the unordered black-note trichord there, {Bb,Ab,Gb}. Example 4.3a presents the relation in a network format, "W" and "B" signifying the white-note and black-note trichords, respectively.

Example 4.3b "retrogrades" the network of example 4.3a. Network b can stand (isographically) for a relation of the first reprise to the second, where "B" and "W" now mean the black-note C# version of the theme and the white-note C version, respectively. Or B and W can stand for the unordered pitch-class sets that project the harmonies for the two reprises: {F,Eb,Db,B,Ab} at the first reprise (m. 65) and {E,D,C,Bb,G} at the second reprise (m. 79). The right-to-left arrow of example 4.3b suggests that the first reprise "returns" to the second; in fact the theme and its harmony at the second reprise do recapitulate the original pitch-class level of mm. 25–29.

Network c cannot be distinguished from network b by any formal features. It only looks different on the page, because the T11 arrow is displayed from left to right and the left/right page-positions of the B and W nodes are reversed. Visually, the graph of network c suggests more an "inversion" of graph a, than a "retrograde." Network c seems more appropriate than network b with regard to our intuition for the harmony of mm. 92–95; there the black-note Db–Ab tremolo is below

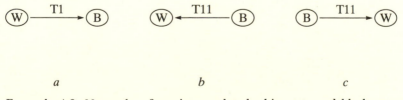

a   *b*   *c*

Example 4.3. Networks of semitone-related white-note and black-note material.

and the C-major music is above, inverting the black/white registral disposition of m. 1 (and of m. 88).

The interconnection between retrograde and inversional structuring, with regard to black/white peripateia, is already manifest in m. 1. The serial layout of the white and black trichords supports hearing the black trichord as a T1-retrograde of the white trichord (example 4.4a); the same layout equally well supports hearing the black as an inversion of the white (example 4.4b). Example 4.4a conveys visually the notion that one trichord precedes the other in time, and that this relation can switch. In addition, its circular structure metaphorically portrays a whirling sparkler at the beginning of the fireworks display. Example 4.4b conveys visually the notion that one trichord lies above and the other below in registral space, and that this relation can switch. The symbol I denotes inversion-about-G-and-A♭, or inversion-about-D-and-D♭.

Example 4.5 shows how the transformational I-motif shapes the music of mm. 87–90. At the climax in m. 87, an I-relation obtains between the extremes of the two glissandos: the A♭ of the right-hand attack is I-balanced by the G of the left-hand release; the A of the left-hand attack is I-balanced by the G♭ of the right-hand release. Over mm. 88–89, the I-balanced F–G–A and B♭–A♭–G♭ trichords both echo the glissandos and recall the opening of the piece.[4] Along

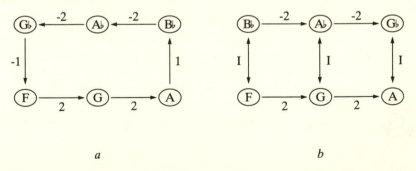

a   *b*

Example 4.4. Retrograde and inversional hearings of the opening trichords.

4. One must admire Debussy's finesse in assigning the black-note glissando of m. 87

Example 4.5. The I-relation shapes the music of mm. 87–90.

with the trichords we hear D♮; in the context of the passage, these recall the D♮ "sparks" of mm. 3ff. The music of mm. 88–89 repeatedly breaks off at these D♮s, seeking a continuation. The structural continuation, as example 4.5 shows, is to the downbeat of m. 90; there the D♮ finds its I-partner, the downbeat D♭. D–D♭ is not just an I-partnership; it is one semitone-center of the inversion. To drive home the progression of D to D♭, the "sparks" return in mm. 96–97, now on D♭, not D.

As the trichords of m. 1 repeat over and over, we hear the black trichord again and again as both a retrograde and an inversion of the white, in the manner of examples 4.4a–b. We therefore become progressively sensitized to the internal structure of each trichord as a retrograde-inversion of itself. The white trichord (retrograde-) inverts into itself about G, the black trichord about A♭. Two more inversion operations are thereby introduced as transformational motifs: J, inversion-about-G; and K, inversion-about-A♭. As a pitch-class operation, K is also inversion-about-D; the "sparking" D and A♭ of mm. 3–6 thus have analytic value as the two centers of K, the inversion associated with the black trichord. That is logical; the sparks fly upward (in register) off the upper trichord.

The white trichord of m. 1 contains G, one of its K-centers. It does not contain D♭, the other K-center. Nor does any "sparking" D♭ occur

---

to the right hand and the white-tone glissando to the left. The assignment puts the weight of the hands on the high A♭ of the right hand and the low G of the left, respectively, subtly emphasizing the dyad {A♭,G}, a center of I-inversion.

in mm. 3–6. (No D♭ of any sort occurs during mm. 1–16.) But, as we have just observed, "sparking" D♭s do indeed occur toward the very end of the piece, and we associate them with the sparking Ds of mm. 3ff. The D♭s at the end of the piece are thus fruitfully heard, inter alia, as representing a center of J.

Pertinent portions of example 4.1 suggest that it is interesting to put the pedal D♭–A♭ tremolo of mm. 90–98 together with the accented G and D from "Aux armes, citoyens!" (mm. 92–93). The D♭ and the G group together as the two centers of J; the A♭ and the D group together as the two centers of K — recalling the right hand of mm. 3–6. There is a T1-relation (not a T11-relation!) between the centers {D♭,G} and the centers {D,A♭}. Regrouping, one also hears that {D♭,D} is a center for I, as is {G,A♭}. We have just heard {D,D♭} as an I-center very strongly, at m. 90 (end of example 4.5); now (at the downbeat of m. 96) the relation is echoed in a pungent verticality. All of this bears on "metastable" aspects of the coda.

Example 4.6 synopsizes pertinent interrelations of I, J, and K in a network that involves the two trichords from m. 1. A♭ and G are each given two nodes for technical reasons that need not concern us here.[5]

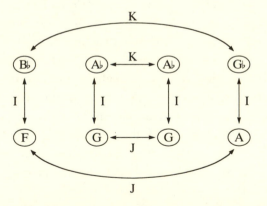

Example 4.6. Various inversional relations involving the opening trichords.

5. If there were only one A♭ node, an arrow from that node to itself would have to be labeled by T0 rather than by K. The awkwardness is caused by the formal requirements of Lewin 1987, section 9.2.2 (pp. 195–96).

108

Starting at any white note, if you follow the J-arrow and then the I-arrow, you will arrive at a certain black note. Starting at the same white note, if you follow the I-arrow and then the K-arrow, you will arrive at the same black note. That illustrates the abstract transformational equation KI = IJ. Following either arrow path, you will notice that the black note at which you arrive is T1 of the white note from which you started. Abstractly: KI = IJ = T1. Similarly, JI = IK = T11.

From those equations we can derive many others involving our motivic transformations T1, T11, I, J, and K. For instance, start with the equation KI = T1,; multiply both sides of the equation on the right by I. The result: K = (T1)(I). That is, if you transpose by 1 the I-inversion of something, the result will be the K-inversion of that thing. Similarly, I = (T1)(J). K, which is (T1)(I), is then (T1)(T1)(J); that is K = (T2)(J). If you transpose by 2 the J-inversion of something, you will obtain the K-inversion of that thing.

An important abstract idea should be noted here explicitly; we shall call it "the J/K symmetry feature." If X is a pitch class set that J-inverts into itself, then T1(X) will K-invert into itself. (And if Y K-inverts into itself, then T11(Y) will J-invert into itself.) The proof may be omitted by a skittish reader.[6] This J/K symmetry feature is manifest in the relations of the white and black trichords within m. 1: X = {F,G,A} J-inverts into itself; T1(X) is {Bb,Ab,Gb} and T1(X) K-inverts into itself.

The J/K symmetry feature can also be observed in the harmonies that support the entrance of the theme (mm. 25–27), the first reprise (m. 65), and the second reprise (m. 79). The theme and the second reprise are both supported by the pitch-class set X = {E,D,C,Bb,G}. The set X J-inverts into itself, as is suggested by the contours of m. 25

---

6. We have already observed that I = (T1)(J). Take the known equation KI = T1; multiply both sides on the left by K. We obtain the equation I = (K)(T1). Thence we infer that (K)(T1) = (T1)(J).

Suppose J(X) = X, as described. Set Y = T1(X); we are to prove that K(Y) = Y. We write: K(Y) = K(T1(X)) = T1(J(X)) [via the equation at the end of the preceding paragraph of this note]. And T1(J(X)) = T1(X) [since J(X) = X]. And T1(X) = Y, Y being so defined. In sum, K(Y) = Y, as asserted.

(first half) and m. 79. The first reprise is harmonzied by the set T1 (X) = {F,E♭,D♭,B,A♭}; that set K-inverts into itself. These relations of (theme to) first reprise to second reprise thereby recapitulate on an expanded time-scale the pertinent J/K symmetry features of (white trichord to) black trichord to white trichord, within m. 1.

We earlier observed the J/K symmetry feature in connection with the music of mm. 92–93. The pedal D♭ and the G at the downbeat of m. 92 are centers of J-inversion; the set X = {D♭,G} J-inverts into itself. T1(X) here is {D,A♭}, a set that K-inverts into itself; this set comprises the two centers of K-inversion. D appears at m. 93; A♭ appears in the pedal bass.

The motivic transformations J, I, and K illustrate what I shall call the "bisection motif"; I "bisects" J and K in the manner of example 4.7a. The T-labels for the arrows mean "(T1)(J) = I"; "(T1)(I) = K"; "(T2)(J) = K." Thus the transformational "distance" T2, from J to K, is bisected into T1 (from J to I) and T1 (from I to K). Example 4.7b generalizes the network of example 4.7a into a bisection graph. Here a generic transformational span w, from the left node to the right node, is bisected into two v-spans: a v-span from left node to center node, and a v-span from center node to right node. The idea generalizes recent conceptions of Jay Rahn (1985, 71–74).

Example 4.8 shows how the bisection motif saturates the foreground of mm. 1–6. Example 4.8a interprets the white trichord in a bisection network; the interval (transpositional distance) from F to A is bisected by G. Example 4.8b gives the analogous interpretation for

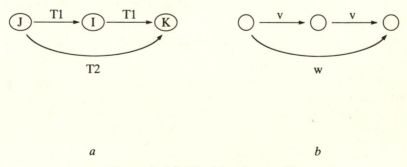

a   *b*

Example 4.7. The bisection motif.

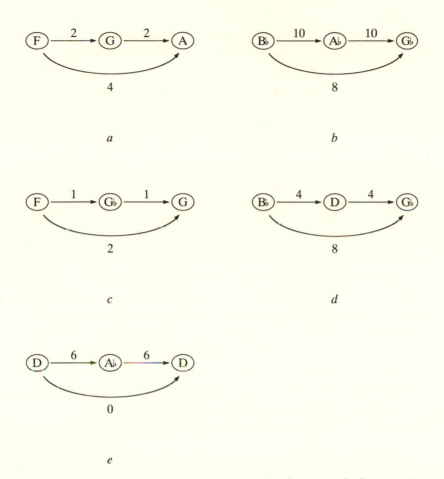

Example 4.8. The bisection motif saturates the foreground of mm. 1–6.

the black trichord, using pitch-class intervals 10 and 8. (One could assert the stronger pitch intervals −2 and −4 here.) Example 4.8b is the negative (mod 12) of example 4.8a; the two networks are isographic. The isography interprets the white/black relationship as inversional.

Example 4.8c shows how the black note G♭ "bisects" the consecutive notes F and G of the white trichord. Similarly, the black note A♭ bisects consecutive white notes G–A, whereas the white note G bisects black notes A♭–G♭ and the white note A bisects black notes B♭–A♭.

This intermeshing character of the black and white notes, each vis-à-vis the other, was observed in the glissandos of the climax at m. 87.

Example 4.8d shows the "sparking" D of mm. 3ff. in a new light. Not only is the D a center of K-inversion; it is a pitch-class bisector for the 8-dyad Bb–Gb. Comparing network 8d to network 8b, we see that the dyad has two pc bisectors. Indeed, any dyad that spans an even interval will have two pc bisectors a tritone apart.[7] The D and Ab sparks on the top staff of mm. 3–6 are thus the two bisectors of the Bb–Gb dyad.

The D and Ab sparks arrange themselves in register so as to project Ab dividing the octave D. Example 4.8e reduces this to a pitch-class bisection of the 0 interval from D to D; Ab bisects the D-to-D "dyad." (D itself is the other formal bisector of that formal dyad.)

Example 4.9 shows the bisection motif at a higher level of organization. The symbols "8a" and so forth refer to the graphs on examples 4.8a–d, ignoring the specific pitch classes involved. Example 4.8c shows an interval of 2 bisected into two intervals of 1; we can refer to that as "1 + 1 = 2." Example 4.8a analogously shows "2 + 2 = 4." The graph on example 4.8a thus multiplies all the intervals of example 4.8c by 2. Hence, example 4.9 subtends an arrow labeled "times 2" between the nodes labeled "8c" and "8a."

Example 4.9. The bisection motif at a higher level of organization.

7. If pc s bisects the dyad ⟨r,t⟩, let i be the interval from r to s; i will then also be the interval from s to t. Let s′ be the pc a tritone from s; then int(r,s′) = i + 6, and int(s′,t) also = i + 6. Thus s′ also bisects r and t.

(Given any bisector of r and t, let j be the interval from r to that bisector. Then j is also the interval from the bisector to t. Hence 2j is the interval from r to t. And int(r,t) = 2i. So 2j = 2i. Hence 2(j − i) = 0 mod 12. It follows that j − 1 is either 0 or 6; thus either j = i or j = i + 6. Hence a bisectable dyad has exactly two bisectors. Dyads that span odd intervals are of course not bisectable.)

Example 4.8d shows intervals "4 + 4 = 8"; this graph multiplies all the intervals of example 4.8a by 2. Example 4.9 therefore subtends another arrow labeled "times 2" between nodes "8a" and "8d." In going from example 4.8c to example 4.8d, intervals are multiplied by 4: "1 + 1 = 2" becomes "4 + 4 = 8." Example 4.8a thus bisects the dyad ⟨8c,8d⟩: "times 4" is bisected into "times 2, times 2."

Example 4.8b is another bisector for the dyad ⟨8c,8d⟩: Here the gesture "times 4" is bisected into the gestures "times −2" and "times −2." The gestures "times 2" and "times −2" are the two "square roots" of the gesture "times 4."[8]

The {C,D} of m.7 introduces an enormous amount of material into the composition. As the lowest event in the piece so far, {C4,D4} is easily grouped with the white-note trichord F4–G4–A4; the low dyad also attacks together with the trichord. The pentatonic formation stands out after the music of mm. 1–6, which projected the chromatic sound of the two trichords plus a certain growing whole-tone character in the upper registers.

In the present context, we can observe first that the C and the D are the "other" bisectors of the white-note trichord, that is, "other" than the G♭ and the A♭ we have already heard so much. F-to-G is bisected not only by G♭ but by C; G-to-A is bisected not only by A♭ but by D. The observation attributes a certain analytic value to {C,D,G♭,A♭}, the set of "white trichord bisectors." That abstract set later materializes in the piece with considerable harmonic autonomy, as at m. 45 (first half), m. 53 (middle), m. 57 (second half), and mm. 76–78 (as the top of the whole-tone pentachord).

The process of bisection thus continues "logically" into m. 7, relating the {C,D} dyad to the white-note trichord. The {C,D} dyad also combines with the black-note trichord, forming a whole-tone pentachord that continues to enlarge the whole-tone sound beyond mm. 3–6. That becomes even clearer when the {C,D} appears in an upper

8. The gestures "times 2" and so forth, when applied to intervals mod 12, do not have inverse gestures. The flow of example 4.9 cannot be retrograded. That distinguishes example 4.9 from other bisection graphs we have so far studied. The mappings "times 2" and so on are homomorphisms, not isomorphisms (or isographies). The distinction is exposed in Lewin 1987, 201–6.

register at m. 8; upper registers are where we have become primed to listen for growing whole-tone sounds. Nevertheless, even the {C,D} dyad of m. 7, an eighth note indicated *marqué*, does sound through the first black-note trichord of the measure.[9] The whole-tone pentachord begins to create pressure toward introducing E, the missing note of the pertinent whole-tone scale and the note that will eventually arrive at the downbeat of m. 25.

Example 4.10 shows an interrelation of pentatonic and whole-tone structures around mm. 7–8 that will recur later in the piece. On the left side of the example, the low {C,D} combines with the lower /024/ trichord to form the pentatonic set PENT = {C,D,F,G,A}. Here {C,D}

WTP above (m. 8);
the major second {C, D} with stem up is T4 above
the upper major second of the upper /024/ trichord.

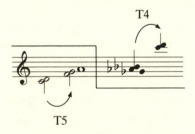

PENT below (m. 7);
the major second {C, D} with stem down is T5 below
the lower major second of the lower /024/ trichord.

Example 4.10. Pentatonic and whole-tone structures in mm. 7–8.

9. A slight half-pedal on the {C,D} can be useful to sustain its sound adequately. Alternately, as I prefer myself, the {C,D} of m. 7 can be played (despite the composer's apparent intention) with the fourth and fifth fingers of the left hand. With some practice, those fingers can project the sort of attack accent indicated; they can then return into their keys before the dampers fall completely, guaranteeing that the full eighth-note duration will not be cheated. Debussy could easily have written the eighth note as a sixteenth plus a sixteenth rest; he did not do so. The eighth note is conspicuously the longest note in the piece so far.

appears T5 below the lower 2-dyad of the trichord. On the right side of the example, the high {C,D} combines with the upper /024/ trichord to form the whole-tone pentachord WTP = {G♭,A♭,B♭,C,D}. Here {C,D} appears T4 above the upper 2-dyad of the trichord. One notes the simultaneous dichotomies of pentatonic/whole-tone, lower/upper, and T5/T4 in this arrangement, along with the pivotal role of the {C,D} dyad.

The {C,D} is Debussy's signature dyad. The indication *marqué* in m. 7 is exquisitely appropriate. The word of course signifies a conventional sort of musical accentuation. But it also has many colloquial nuances that fit particularly strongly with the signature motif. The piece is "branded" with Debussy's signature. It is something he "has written" to us, "pointing something out" to us (*qu'il nous a marqué*). The idea of an admonitory message will come out very strongly in the *Marseillaise* citation, as discussed earlier.

PENT = {C,D,F,G,A} J-inverts into itself, as does the signature dyad {C,D}. The power of J is thus on the rise over mm. 7–10. WTP = {G♭,A♭,B♭,C,D} does not K-invert into itself; the subset {G♭,A♭,B♭,D}, which saturated the upper register of mm. 3–6 and will again saturate the upper register of mm. 11–14, does K-invert into itself. The new note C, heard in WTP, disrupts the K-inversional balance of the whole-tone structuring. To restore that balance, we need the K-partner of C, that is, the note E. Pressure toward the eventual E arrival of m. 25 is built up by this means; we already noted pressure toward E as completing the whole-tone scale from WTP. The low A♭ of m. 7 meanwhile keeps one of the K-centers weighty, in the bass.

The sense of building pressure passes into foreground textural aspects of the music during mm. 11–16. D and A♭ sparks shoot off at twice their earlier rate during mm. 11–14; a crescendo starts at m. 12. The crescendo gathers impetus at m. 15, where the white and black trichords suddenly rocket upwards; in this context mm. 15–16 build further tension because they form a two-measure group after the regular four-measure groups of mm. 3–6, 7–10, and 11–14.

The first climactic contour apex of the piece is then attained at the downbeat of m. 17, and energy dissipates during the registral and dynamic descent that follows. The achievement of m. 17 is only provisional, as the three-measure group tells us (mm. 17–19). In particular, we do not get an E-downbeat. Example 4.11 sketches some of the things we do get.

On example 4.11a, we see how the white-note J-symmetrical pentatonic set PENT can be heard moving by T1, at m. 17, to the black-note K-symmetrical pentatonic set T1(PENT). The move suggests a retrograde relation in the serial orderings of the pentachords. It manifests the J/K symmetry feature: PENT J-inverts into itself; T1 (PENT) K-inverts into itself. In all these respects, the relations of PENT and T1(PENT) on example 4.11a expand relations already explored between the white-note and black-note trichords. In particular, as the white-note trichord moves up by T1 to the black-note trichord in the example, the signature dyad {C,D} also moves up by T1 to {D♭,E♭}.

Example 4.11b explores another relation between the white-note PENT of mm. 7ff. and the black-note pentatonic set of m. 17 — specifically, an inversional relationship. Just as the black-note trichord is the I-inversion of the white-note trichord, so the black-note pentatonic set is the I-inversion of PENT. The signature dyad {C,D} I-inverts into {E♭,D♭}.

It is no coincidence that both alternate analyses of examples 4.11a and 4.11b obtain here, just as the "T1-relation" and the "I-relation" both obtain between the white trichord and the black trichord. That is a necessary aspect of the J/K symmetry feature. Specifically, if X is any pcset that J-inverts into itself, then [T1(X) K-inverts into itself and] X I-inverts into T1(X): that is, $T1(X) = I(X)$.[10]

Example 4.11c synopsizes in a new way some of the J/K motifs we have been discussing. The first two stems-up events of the example show the J-symmetrical white trichord moving up to the K-symmetrical black trichord via T1. The stem-down D under the second event of the example represents the "sparking" Ds of mm. 3ff.; here D is a center of K-inversion, so the entire second verticality of the example

10. Proof: We know that $I = (T1)J$. Hence $I(X) = T1(J(X))$. Substituting $J(X) = X$, we obtain $I(X) = T1(X)$, as asserted.

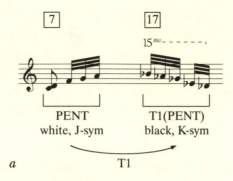

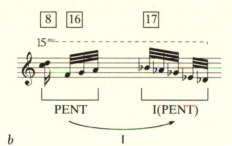

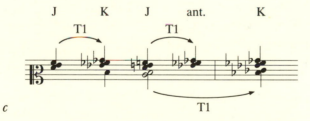

Example 4.11. Transformational motifs discharging at the downbeat of m. 17.

is K-symmetrical. The third verticality puts {C,D} under the white trichord, as at m. 7 in the music; this projects the J-symmetrical PENT. The fourth verticality represents the prolonged power of {C,D} (especially in the sparking upper register) together with the black trichord. As already observed, this WTP sonority is not K-symmetrical; it generates a certain pressure toward E, the K-partner of C, which would complete the whole-tone scale. But the downbeat of m. 17 works differently, as displayed by the last verticality of example 4.11c. K-symmetry is indeed reestablished, with a registral, rhythmic, and dynamically climactic local effect. But the K-symmetry is not created by an E-arrival. Rather, as the black-note trichord from the preceding structural verticality is maintained, the {C,D} dyad moves up via T1 to {Db,Eb}, completing the T1-move from PENT to T1(PENT) in this syncopated fashion: first the trichord, then the dyad. In this sketch, the power of the downbeat is carried not by the high Bb or the black trichord, but by the T1-move from the signature dyad {C,D} to the new 2-dyad {Db,Eb}.

The beginning of example 4.12 reproduces that T1 move, and then shows how the {Cb,Db} dyad of mm. 18–19 executes the complementary or inverse T11-move from {C,D}; the connection in register is very strong from m. 7 to mm. 18–19. Taking a hint from the idea of "complementation" here, let us imagine, instead of the T11 arrow on the example, a T1 arrow running from right to left, from {Cb,Db} (mm. 18–19) to {C,D} (m. 7). We shall then hear a bisection schema at work: {Cb,Db} is to {C,D} (via T1) as {C,D} is to {Db,Eb} (via T1). Thus the 2-interval by which {Cb,Db} lies under {Db,Eb} is artic-

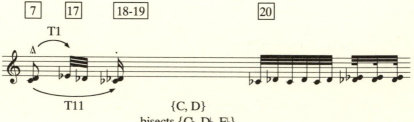

Example 4.12. {C,D} bisects the new trichord {Cb,Db,Eb}.

ulated into "2 = 1 + 1." And a new whole-tone trichord {Cb,Db,Eb} is introduced. The signature dyad {C,D}, which was introduced as the "fifth-bisectors" of {F,G,A} at m. 7, is now manifest as the "semitone bisectors" of {Cb,Db,Eb}.

The {Cb,Db,Eb} trichord is only a theoretical inference on the left side of example 4.12, through m. 19. At m. 20 and following, as shown on the right side of the example, the inferred trichord materializes in the foreground of the music.

After what one might suppose a climactic triumph of K-inversion at m. 17, along the lines of example 4.11c, the rebounding {Cb,Db} dyads of mm. 18–19 make an awkward effect, for they set up the {Cb,Db,Eb} trichord as just discussed, and that trichord is J-symmetrical, as is the set of its semitone-bisectors [C,D]. Thus, instead of confirming the K-downbeat, mm. 18–19 yank us back to J-structuring, which continues into mm. 20ff. The yank is further accented by the entrance of the pitch class Cb in m. 18; Cb is the eleventh note of the total chromatic to appear in the piece so far. The rhetoric of the gesture is worth noting: an ostensible and conventionally approached acoustic "climax" is set up at m. 17, and then an even stronger structural point of arrival supervenes in its aftermath. One notes the rhetorical parallel with the gigantic acoustic climax at m. 87, followed by the devastating arrival of the *Marseillaise* in the coda, after "it is all over."

Example 4.12 indicates that the trichord {Cb,Db,Eb}, over m. 20ff. is in a sense a sister trichord to {F,G,A}: both whole-tone trichords are bisected by the signature dyad {C,D}. In that sense, the sister trichord to {Bb,Ab,Gb} is {E,D,C}. Until m. 17 we have heard F–G–A leading over and over to the answering Bb–Ab–Gb. The sister progression would then have Cb–Db–Eb leading to an answering E–D–C. Once again, and in a new way, pressure rises for an arrival on E, now an arrival specifically on the motive-form E–D–C. The previously heard progression of F–G–A to Bb–Ab–Gb, plus the anticipated sister progression of Cb–Db–Eb to E–D–C, forms a serial derivation on the total chromatic. It is interesting, in that connection, that Cb appears as the eleventh note of the total chromatic just at the moment when the trichord Cb–Db–E begins to form.

Of course E, the last note of the total chromatic to appear, arrives at m. 25 within the trichord E–D–C. The trichord C♭–D♭–E♭ builds up directly to that downbeat over mm. 20–24, and the last beat of m. 24 plus the first three notes of m. 25 features exactly the progression C♭–D♭–E♭ to E–D–C across the double bar, at the very highest registral level in the piece so far. The serial derivation holds water because one hears this "apex" moment as analogous — in rhythm, texture, and contour — to the earlier provisional apex of m. 17. There we heard the first half of the derivation: F–G–A progressing to B♭–A♭–G♭.[11]

During mm. 20–24 the bisecting divider C appears as an accessory tone for the C♭–D♭–E♭ trichord, but the bisecting divider D does not. The Cs suggest the "missing" trichord E–D–C, whereas the locally missing Ds, like the as-yet-completely-unheard E, intensify our desire to hear the E–D–C trichord in its entirety. The Cs of mm. 20–24 (without any Ds) also connect the middle C of m. 7 with the middle C of the theme at mm. 27ff. Though the recurrent Cs of mm. 20–24 "dissonate" against the C♭–D♭–E♭ trichord, they anticipate the outburst of C root-sensation over m. 25 and the theme to come. In that respect one can compare the effect to the "dissonant" tympani roll on C at the end of the scherzo in Beethoven's Fifth Symphony, leading into the Finale.

The first two verticalities of example 4.13 show the J-symmetrical

Example 4.13. Expansion of J-symmetrical sonorities over mm. 7–25.

11. It was clever of Debussy to put the "sparking" C7 and D7 into the upper register of the piece at m. 8. The B♭6 of m. 17 does not get so high even though it is a local apex of the large contour. Only with the E♭7 of m. 24 do we go above the earlier D7, and then the E7 of m. 25 goes even higher immediately thereafter. That makes the downbeat of m. 25 sound very high, in addition to its other accented features.

signature dyad {C,D} of m. 7 expanding into the J-symmetrical tri-chord {Cb,Db,Eb} of mm. 17–19 and mm. 20ff. This follows the schema of example 4.12: {C,D} comprises the semitone bisectors of {Cb,Db,Eb}. The next stage of example 4.13 shows the process con-tinuing, as the trichord expands to produce the J-symmetrical tetra-chord {Bb,C,D,E}. {Cb,Db,Eb} comprises the semitone bisectors of {Bb,C,D,E}. The tetrachord is part of the structural downbeat har-mony at m. 25; the rest of that harmony is the note G, which is shown on the right of example 4.13. G ties off the scheme of example 4.13, as a center of J-inversion — so indicated with an open notehead on the example. That aspect of the G suggests one analytic value for the G in the incipit horn call of the theme, at m. 27. The harmony of m. 25 will be called APEX; sets and supersets of this set class saturate much of the piece from m. 25 on.

Theme and Variations (mm. 25–46)

Example 4.14 analyzes the melodies of the theme, and of three variations, into incipit, middle, and ending sections. Rhythm and texture at the end of variation 2 are appropriate for "ending" mate-rial; this measure elides into the incipit of variation 3. So far as inter-vallic structure is concerned, the same material actually extends the middle of variation 2: in m. 44 {Bb,Fb,Gb} moves by T1 into {B,F,G}; the latter then moves by T1 into the "ending" notes {C,Gb,Ab} of m. 45. The move by T1-and-T1-again is familiar.

In the theme, and again in variation 1, the last note of the middle section lies a whole tone above the first note of the incipit. The ending section reprises the incipit, bringing the whole-tone neighbor back down. In these respects, variation 2 departs from the behavior of the theme and of variation 1. On the other hand, the incipit of variation 2 itself includes the whole-tone upper neighbor to its opening note, and we hear the neighboring C return to Bb twice, once at the downbeat of m. 43, and again at m. 44. (The pianist must take heed not to cheat the Cs at the end of m. 42 and the end of m. 43!)

The trichord {C,Ab,Gb}, which has to do double duty as ending for variation 2 and as incipit for variation 3, is called on for even further

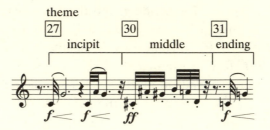

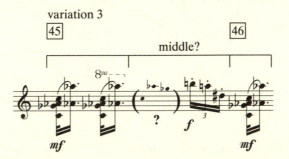

Example 4.14. The melodies of the theme and of three variations parse into incipit, middle, and ending sections.

duty, launching the middle section of variation 3. It must then serve as "ending" for variation 3 and as "incipit" for the aborted repetition of variation 3 that begins in m. 46. (The repetition never reaches its "ending.") The trichord is supported by D in the bass; the total harmony in the first half of m. 45 is {C,D,Gb,Ab}. As noted earlier, this set comprises the two bisector dyads of F–G–A — that is, the semitone bisectors {Gb,Ab} along with the signature fifth-bisectors {C,D}.

The T1-and-then-again-T1 motif, already noted in the middle and ending of variation 2, is manifest in the incipit and middle of the theme. Here T1 bisects T2 and C♯ bisects the melodic signature dyad C–D. The large-scale melodic gesture is C (incipit) to D (end of middle section) and then back to C (ending); the whole-tone neighboring gesture uses the signature dyad to elaborate the local root C. In this context the C♯ (beginning of middle section), bisecting C–D, is a passing tone at a lower level.

The opening interval of the theme is a rising fifth; variation 1 opens with a tritone and variation 2 with a fourth. In the theme, and again in variations 1 and 2, both the bottom and the top notes of the opening interval are subsequently elaborated by their upper whole-tone neighbors. (Note again the Cs in mm. 42–43).

Example 4.15 elaborates those observations into a structural sketch with commentary. Using the sketch, we can hear a transformational source for the successively contracting incipit intervals. The lower notes of those intervals move up by successive T5 leaps, from C at m. 27 to F at m. 35 to Bb at m. 42. Meanwhile, the upper notes of the incipit intervals move up by successive T4 leaps, from G at m. 27 to Cb at m. 35 to Eb at m. 42.

All those notes, on their T5 or T4 journeys, are accompanied by their whole-tone upper neighbors. Example 4.15 thus portrays a chain of major seconds with downward stems, a chain moving up by T5 leaps from the (signature CD of the) theme to variation 1 and thence to variation 2. The overall result is the complete pentatonic set {C,D,F,G,Bb}, which is T5(PENT). Likewise, the example portrays a chain of major seconds with upward stems, a chain moving up by T4 leaps from the theme to variation 1 and thence to variation 2.

T5(WT) above (notes with stems up);
the major seconds with stems up rise by successive T4s
from the theme to variation 1 to variation 2

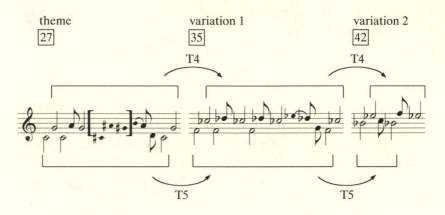

Example 4.15. Pentatonic and whole-tone structures in the melodic line of mm. 27–43.

T5(PENT) below (notes with stems down);
the major seconds with stems down rise by successive T5s
from the theme to variation 1 to variation 2

The overall result is the complete whole-tone set {G,A,B,D♭,E♭,F}. The set is labeled "T5(WT)" on the example because variation 1, both on the sketch and in the music, comprises exactly the notes of the subset {F,G,B,D♭,E♭}, and that whole-tone pentachord is T5(WTP). The analytic labels thereby produce the idea of whole-tone versus pentatonic structuring, all at the "T5 level."

The idea comports well with example 4.10, which displayed the original source of whole-tone versus pentatonic structuring in mm. 7–10. The layout and commentary for both examples 4.10 and 4.15 are designed to bring out the structural resemblances. One notes on example 4.15, as on example 4.10, "the simultaneous dichotomies of pentatonic/whole-tone, lower/upper, and T5/T4 in this arrangement." The {C,D} dyad appears at the lower left of both examples.

Example 4.16 tries to emphasize the structural resemblances of

The networks to the left correlate with example 4.10.
The networks to the right correlate with example 4.15.

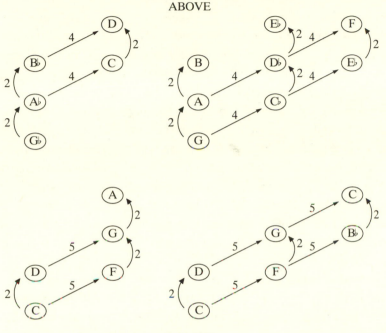

Example 4.16. Structural resemblances between examples 4.10 and 4.15.

examples 4.10 and 4.15 in a compact format. Registral, not temporal, ordering is used for the "2"-intervals from Gb to Ab and from Ab to Bb.

Example 4.15 displays bisection motifs in its transformational layout (which example 4.10 did not). Specifically, the stems-up part of the example displays a "4 + 4 = 8" gesture that carries G (theme) through Cb (variation 1) to Eb (variation 2). Likewise, the stems-down part of the example displays a "5 + 5 = 10" gesture that carries C (theme) through F (variation 1) to Bb (variation 2). We recognize the "4 + 4 = 8" gesture as one previously encountered at m. 3, where the 8-dyad B♭–G♭ was bisected into the two 4-dyads B♭–D and D–G♭ by the D "spark"; that was the beginning of "whole-tone sound" in the piece. "5 + 5 = 10" is the inversion of "7 + 7 = 2"; that relation was first heard at m. 7, where C bisected the 2-dyad F–G into two 7-dyads F–C and C–G, while D bisected G–A into the 7-dyads G–D and D–A. That was the beginning of "pentatonic sound" in the piece.

The idea of whole-tone versus pentatonic structuring, indicated so strongly on the melodic sketch of example 4.15, is amply audible in the harmonic character of the corresponding music. The theme contains a pentatonic harmony, when the cell C–A–G of the incipit sounds against the running E–D–C trichords of the accompaniment (m. 29); the effect is transposed through the middle section of the theme in m. 30. Variation 1 is completely whole-tone in sound, projecting the pentachord T5(WTP) in both melody and harmony. The opening of variation 2 features a pentatonic subset in the melody, with diatonic harmony. The opening of variation 3 is again a whole-tone subset.

The next four examples investigate the harmony of mm. 25–46 more carefully, paying special attention to large-scale transformational gestures and motifs. Example 4.17 covers the span of the theme (mm. 25–34). Over mm. 25–29 the example asserts the J-symmetrical APEX harmony already discussed. The pitch class A, appearing in

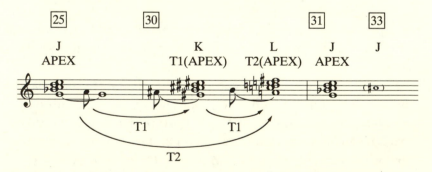

Example 4.17. Transformational profile and inversional symmetries of APEX-forms, mm. 25–33.

the melodic cell C–A–G of m. 29, is analyzed here as an accessory tone to the G of the APEX set.[12]

During m. 30, APEX rises to T1(APEX), which rises to T2(APEX). This prominent feature of the harmony works in parallel with the rise of the melody in the lower register from C through C# to D. On example 4.17, the thematic rise is portrayed by an arrow graph with the familiar profile T1-and-T1-make-T2. T1(APEX) is K-symmetrical — exhibiting the familiar J/K symmetry feature. T2(APEX) is "L-symmetrical," where L denotes inversion-about-A, or inversion-about-Eb. As one hears clearly from the example, L is to K as K is to J. The intuition can be supplemented by appropriate mathematical formulas.[13]

At m. 31 the theme returns to C–G for its ending segment, and the harmony returns in parallel to the J-symmetrical APEX. Then, over the interlude of mm. 33–34, the figuration adds a C#. In the context, C# has strong analytic value as the other center of J-inversion (in addition to the G already present). The span of example 4.17 thus articulates a gesture that proceeds from J-symmetry through K-symmetry to L-symmetry, followed by a return to J-symmetry.

Example 4.18 sketches a transformational interpretation for the harmony from the end of the theme to the interlude following variation 1. The overall gesture is a single T1, taking the J-symmetrical APEX harmony of m. 31 to the K-symmetrical T1(APEX) embedded within m. 39. The gesture is familiar from the left side of example 4.17. Example 4.18 diminutes the same progression by staggering the semitone motions within the individual "voices" of the harmony; the

12. We earlier mentioned the secondary set T7(PENT) that appears here when the C–A–G cell is melded with the C–D–E trichord of the accompaniment (ignoring the Bb of APEX). T7(PENT) does not emerge into the foreground of the music until it recurs at the *Marseillaise* citation in the coda. In the context of mm. 25–30 one hesitates to assign it high analytic priority.

13. Any formula derived earlier that involves J and K remains true if K and L are respectively substituted for J and K throughout. For instance, (T1)(K) = (L)(T1). All of the J/K symmetry features become K/L symmetry features when the same substitutions are made. For inversion I, one must substitute inversion "H," inversion-about-D-and-Eb or inversion-about-Ab-and-A.

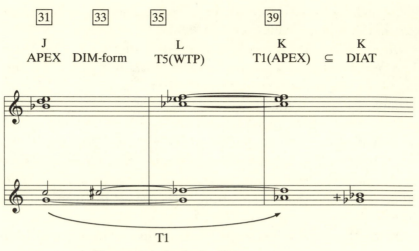

Example 4.18. Transformational profile of mm. 31–39, with "passing" DIM-
and WTP-forms.

syncopated voice-leading gives rise to intermediate harmonies DIM
and T5(WTP). The latter pcset has already been discussed; it completely saturates variation 1 in the melody as well as the harmony,
and it expands, as T5(WT), to govern the "stems-up" portion of
example 4.15. The set is L-symmetrical, as indicated on example 4.18.

The set {G,Bb,C#,D,E}, comprising a "diminished seventh chord"
plus one more tone, has not been mentioned before. It is marked as
a "DIM-form" on example 4.18; a prime level for the set class will be
asserted later in the analysis. In example 4.18 the C# of the DIM-
form displaces the C of APEX, beginning the T1-push from APEX
to T1(APEX) that will finally conclude at m. 39. On example 4.17,
the C# of m. 33 simply adjoined itself to APEX, as an extra J-center,
without displacing the C. That was a different context. Measure 33
appears in an interlude. Looking backward over the theme, we see
that the C# of example 4.17 stabilizes J-inversion and does not dis-
lodge C♮; looking forward toward variation 1 and the next interlude,
we see that the C# of example 4.18 moves C to anticipate the harmony
of variation 1 and the harmony of the next interlude thereafter. "The

C# of example 4.17" and "the C# of example 4.18" are different phenomenological objects, inhabiting different regions of phenomenological space/time.[14]

As example 4.18 shows, the K-symmetrical T1(APEX) of m. 39 joins with the (K-symmetrical) dyad {G♭,B♭} to form the seven-note diatonic set, marked "DIAT." The analysis may at first seem somewhat forced, carving T1(APEX) out of the diatonic set because we "need" it for the big arrow of example 4.18. But there is much in the music to help articulate the diatonic set of m. 39 in this way. For one thing, m. 39 is a big registral "apex" moment, the first such moment since m. 25. The first note of m. 39, the apex note F7, is the highest pitch of the piece so far; it lies in a T1 relation to the apex note E7 of m. 25. That relation is manifest on example 4.18 in the T1-relation between the top notes for APEX and T1(APEX). Furthermore, the first four notes of m. 39, F7–E♭7–D♭7–C♭7, elaborate the T1-relation to m. 25, where the first four notes were E7–D7–C7–B♭6. That relation is manifest on example 4.18, in the T1-relation there between the top four notes of APEX and the top four notes of T1(APEX).

The dyad {G♭,B♭} in m. 39, isolated by the analysis of example 4.18, is to some extent simply the difference between DIAT and T1(APEX). But we can also hear the dyad as the boundary dyad of the original "black trichord" {G♭,A♭,B♭}. DIAT is a maximally black diatonic set. That is, it includes the black-note pentatonic set. We have already heard the black-note pentatonic set in the music at m. 17, where it was specifically heard as an expansion of the black-note trichord. Example 4.11a showed how the black-note pentatonic set came from the earlier white-note PENT via a T1-relation, expanding the T1-relation between the opening white and black trichords of the

---

14. The source of these remarks lies in my article on music theory and phenomenology (Lewin 1986). We all have a certain ingrained tendency to worry how "the" C# can be doing several things "at the same time." There is not one C# but several C#s, including "the C# of m. 33 in example. 4.17" and "the C# of m. 33 in example 4.18." Examples 4.17 and 4.18 are not happening "at the *same* time," whatever we mean by "time."

Octatonic ramifications of DIM, as the piece develops, illustrate many matters discussed in Forte (1991).

piece. And example 4.11c analyzed the T1-move from PENT to T1(PENT) as broken up via voice-leading syncopation; this gave rise to a transitional "anticipatory" whole-tone pentachord on example 4.11c. The voice-leading on example 4.18, from APEX to T1(APEX), likewise breaks up into voice-leading syncopation, which again gives rise to a transitional "anticipatory" whole-tone pentachord on example 4.18.

Measure 17 supports m. 39 as a "black-note" event in yet another way: m. 17 is the only other big "apex" moment so far besides m. 39 and m. 25 (already discussed in this connection). The local apex at m. 17 projected black-note pentatonic music featuring T1(PENT) as an expansion of {B♭,A♭,G♭}. Furthermore, the black-note pentatonic set of m. 17 expanded to a diatonic hexachord at mm. 18–19, when {C♭,D♭} followed the black-note glissando on the rebound. The black-note diatonic hexachord then plausibly expands to the black-note diatonic heptachord of m. 39, all moored around the opening diatonic trichord B♭–A♭–G♭ as point of origin. The foreground figuration of m. 39 indeed puts the trichord into a certain relief. So the {B♭,G♭} dyad of example 4.18, representing the boundaries of the trichord, is plausibly articulated as a subset of DIAT there. It would be equally plausible — perhaps better — to articulate DIAT into T1(APEX) plus the entire black-note trichord {B♭,A♭,G♭}, allowing the tone A♭ to participate in both overlapping subsets of DIAT. A♭ is one center of the local K-symmetry. It receives emphasis in the bass of m. 40.

DIAT is the complement of the pentatonic set T7(PENT) = {A,G} + {C,D,E}. We have already mentioned T7(PENT) in connection with the music of m. 29 (foot-note 12 expanded that discussion). Example 4.19 shows how DIAT is not just a complement but also an expansion of T7(PENT): the {C,D,E} of T7(PENT) expands to the whole-tone tetrachord F–E♭–D♭–C♭ of DIAT; C, D, and E are the semitone bisectors of that tetrachord. Similarly, the A and the G of T7(PENT) are the semitone bisectors of {B♭,A♭,G♭}, the black whole-tone trichord that appears as a marked subset of DIAT. All sets participating in the expansion process — T7(PENT), {C,D,E}, {A,G}, DIAT, {F,E♭,D♭,C♭}, and {B♭,A♭,G♭} — are K-symmetrical. An extra (K-center) A♭ could be added at the end of example 4.19 to represent the

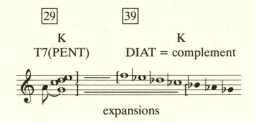

expansions

Example 4.19. The pentatonic subset of
m. 29 expands to its diatonic complement
at m. 39.

A♭ of T1(APEX) along with the whole-tone tetrachord. In all these respects example 4.19 bears fruitful comparison with example 4.13. The earlier example showed an expansion process going from white through black back to white, terminating at the apex of m. 25. Example 4.19 shows an expansion process going from white to black, terminating at the apex of m. 39.

Example 4.20 sketches a harmonic progression for the span of mm. 39–46. This takes us from the interlude before variation 2 through the end of variation 3, and thus through the end of the variations section in the piece.[15] Example 4.20b presents a large profile for the progression, showing a T5-chain of APEX-forms. T1(APEX), at m. 39, is the T5-bisector of T8(APEX) (m. 41) and T6(APEX) (m. 44). T1(APEX) at the beginning of the example progresses to T11(APEX) at the end of the example, via the gesture of T5-and-T5-again. We explored T5-and-T5 again governing the stems-down portion of example 4.15, a melodic gesture that arrived at mm. 42–43; the T5-and-T5-again of example 4.20b carries on the transformational motif in the harmony of mm. 44–46.

Example 4.20a elaborates the harmonic framework of example 4.20b. T1(APEX) and T8(APEX) are embedded in their respective diatonic sets, DIAT and T7(DIAT). On the example, the sets of

15. The spans of examples 4.17, 4.18, and 4.20 take roughly commensurate amounts of time, give or take some fuzziness about their boundaries.

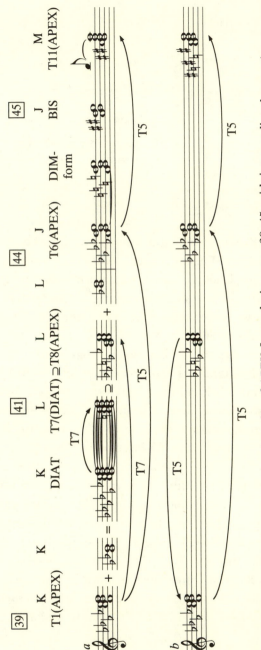

Example 4.20. Transformational profile of APEX-forms during mm. 39–45, with intermediate harmonies.

mm. 39–40 are noted as K-symmetrical, the sets of mm. 41–43 as L-symmetrical.[16]

At m. 44, the set T6(APEX) is J-symmetrical.[17] The motion from T6(APEX) (m. 44) to T11(APEX) (second half of m. 45), portrayed by a T5-arrow on example 4.20b, is diminuted on example 4.20a. The diminution works mostly by rising semitones in the voice-leading. One hears particularly strongly in the melody of m. 44 the leading of {B♭,G♭,F♭} to {B,G,F}, and thence to {C,A♭,G♭} at the beginning of m. 45. In the second half of m. 45, {C,A♭} moves in register to {C♯,A} while G♭ remains, respelled as F♯. Other semitonal features of the voice-leading are D♭-to-D from the first half of m. 44 to the second half, and D-to-D♯ from the first half of m. 45 to the second half.

The rising semitones in the voice-leading do not interact structurally with the overall T5 gesture from T6(APEX) to T11(APEX). They do, however, recall the rising semitones in the voice-leading of mm. 31–39, as depicted on example 4.18. In both passages a large-scale progression from one APEX-form to another is diminuted by rising semitone voice-leading. In both passages, too, the voice leading gives rise to well-articulated transitional harmonies. On example 4.18, the transition from one APEX-form to another proceeds through a DIM-form and then through a whole-tone sonority. On example 4.20, mm. 44–46, the transition from one APEX-form to another also proceeds through a DIM-form and then through a whole-tone sonority.[18]

16. That is a necessary corollary of K/L symmetry. Specifically, if a set X is K-symmetrical, then the set T7(X) must be L-symmetrical. Proof: We know that T1(X) is L-symmetrical. [The argument is analogous to that for J/K symmetry.] Now the operation T6 commutes with the operation L: (L)(T6) = (T6)(L). [T6 commutes with any inversion operation.] Hence L(T7(X)) = L(T6(T1(X)) = T6(L(T1(X))) = T6(T1(X)) [since T1(X) is L-symmetrical], and T6(T1(X)) is T7(X). In sum, L(T7)(X)) = T7(X), as asserted.

17. That is a necessary consequence of APEX's being J-symmetrical. Since the operation T6 commutes with all inversion operations — J in particular — we can write J(T6(APEX)) = T6(J(APEX)) = T6(APEX) [substituting APEX for J(APEX)]. In sum, J(T6(APEX)) = T6(APEX). T6(APEX) is J-symmetrical.

18. It is possible to squeeze a little more similarity out of the correspondences between examples 4.18 and 4.20. But I do not feel that the extra effort repays the analytic work. The overridingly strong aspect of the correspondence is that both

The DIM-form in the second half of m. 44 inverts the DIM-form of m. 33 about E and F (or about B♭ and B). I have not found much analytic substance in that observation. Later, our analysis will assert a prime DIM-form whose transformational peripateia do impose clear structuring on later parts of the piece.

The whole-tone set in the first half of m. 45 is marked "BIS" on example 4.20; it comprises the bisectors of the original white-note trichord {F,G,A}. The {G♭,A♭} of BIS are the semitone bisectors of the trichord (as in m. 1); the {C,D} of BIS are the fifth-bisectors (as in m. 7). The special analytic value of this tetrachord was mentioned earlier.

On the right side of example 4.20, the goal set T11(APEX) is M-symmetrical. "M" here denotes inversion-about-C, or inversion-about-F♯. The M-symmetry marks a strong boundary for the end of the entire theme-and-variations section, that is, mm. 25–46. Reviewing examples 4.17–20, we see that all pcsets in the harmony over mm. 25–46 are inversionally symmetrical except for the two DIM-forms. Furthermore, all those sets are either J-symmetrical, K-symmetrical, or L-symmetrical. The operations J, K, and L enter into a special relationship manifest on example 4.17: J is to K as K is to L. The new operation M interacts with that relationship: M is to J as J is to K as K is to L. M thus extends the J/K relationship "below" J, just as L extended the J/K relationship "above" K. Fancifully speaking, we might say that M explores the "subdominant" side of the J/K relation just as L explored the "dominant" side. The fanciful metaphors accord well with the circle-of-fifths structure audible in the display of example 4.20b.

T11(APEX), on the right side of example 4.20, is also a counterpoise to the powerful T1(APEX) on the left side of that example. T11(APEX) balances T1(APEX) about APEX itself. One could say that APEX bisects T1(APEX) and T11(APEX) in a "T11 and T11 again = T10" arrangement. T6(APEX) is then "the other bisector" for T1(APEX) and T11(APEX), as seen on example 4.20b, where the

---

passages fill the pattern APEX-form, DIM-form, whole-tone set, APEX-form, while proceeding essentially through rising semitone voice-leading.

arrows from m. 39 through m. 44 to the second half of 45 bisect T1(APEX) and T11(APEX) in a "T5 and T5 again = T10" arrangement. In any case, the overall chronological progression of example 4.20b is via T10, from T1(APEX) at m. 39 to T11(APEX) at mm. 45–46.

Episode 1 (mm. 47–56)

Measures 47–48 condense and develop the ideas just mentioned. As seen in example 4.21, T11(APEX), continuing from mm. 45–46, moves back up to T1(APEX), which then moves back down to T11(APEX) via T10. T10 expands into T10-and-T10-again as T11(APEX) moves on to T9(APEX) via T10. T11(APEX) on example 4.21 is thus flanked by its upper T2-transform and its lower T10-transform. The voices move mostly in parallel; the transformational structure of the example is particularly audible in its essential upper voice A–B–A–G.[19] The whole-tone appoggiaturas of the example, B–A, C♯–B, and so forth, add further T10-diminutions to the foreground of the music.

At m. 49 the APEX harmonies give way to DIM-forms, as catalogued by the open noteheads on Example 4.22. The appoggiaturas

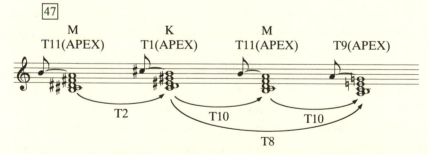

Example 4.21. Transformational profile of APEX-forms during mm. 47–48.

19. One exception to the parallel voice-leading is the frozen {C♯,D♯} dyad of m. 47, which does not move up acoustically to {D♯,E♯} when T1(APEX) appears. The frozen {C♯,D♯} recalls mm. 20–24 to my ear, but I do not grasp a compositional point to that reference.

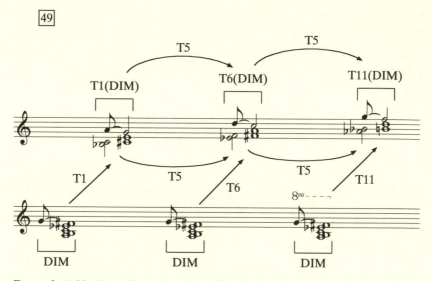

Example 4.22. Transformational profile of DIM-forms during mm. 49–52.

on the example, written as filled-in noteheads with flags, are analyzed as non-chordal in this connection.

The first harmony of m. 49 is asserted as the prime form for DIM in the piece. That is partly because DIM-forms become transformationally mobile only here. It is also because the "DIM" of example 4.22 was characteristic within the melody of variation 3. Indeed, the entire melody of variation 3 (mm. 45–46 on example 4.14) is formed from six pitch classes that project exactly the prime form of DIM, {C,G♭,B,A,D♯}, along with an inverted DIM-form {C,G♭,A♭,A,D♯}. The hexachord suggests that DIM will expand in an octatonic direction.

A further reason for asserting the first harmony of m. 49 as a prime form for DIM is its close resemblance to the harmony T11(APEX), the harmony that governed the transition from the end of the variation section to the opening of episode 1. The end of example 4.20 can be reviewed in this connection together with example 4.21. DIM can be derived from T11(APEX) by substituting C♮ for C♯. That substitution is reasonably audible at the downbeat of m. 49, after the T11(APEX) harmonies of mm. 47–48.

On example 4.22, the prime form of DIM, on the lower staff,

alternates with various transposed forms of DIM on the upper staff. The transposed forms progress via T5-and-T5-again, from T1(DIM) through T6(DIM) to T11(DIM). The major seconds with stems down on the example progress through a pentatonic formation; this recalls the structure of example 4.15. The major seconds with stems up also progress through a pentatonic formation — indeed, through PENT itself.

DIM goes up an octave at mm. 51–52; that makes the T11 relation between DIM and T11(DIM) especially prominent to the ear. We shall have much to say about this.

Example 4.23 sketches the progression of DIM to T11(DIM) and indicates the prolongation of T11(DIM) through mm. 53–54. The stems-up trichords of example 4.23 refer to a familiar progression; example 4.24 indicates the relationship. The left side of example 4.24 shows an ordering for the trichords that is consistent with example

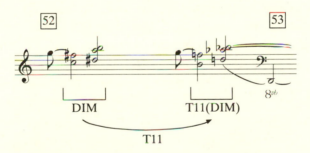

Example 4.23. During mm. 52–54, DIM moves to a prolonged T11(DIM).

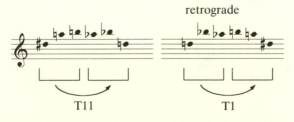

Example 4.24. The upper trichords of example 4.23 derive from an earlier melody.

4.23. When retrograded, as on the right side of example 4.24, that ordering is familiar as a transposed version of the melody from the middle section of variation 3 (m. 44, example 4.14). Example 4.25 constructs a through-line from m. 44 to m. 53 on the basis of such trichords. We can follow a line of chromatically rising minor sixths from {Bb,Gb} and {B,G} in m. 44 to {C,Ab} and {C#,A} in mm. 45–46. The next stage in that process would be {D,Bb}. The {D,Bb} dyad does not appear, however, at m. 47. Rather, the chain of rising sixths overshoots its mark in the second half of m. 45 and of m. 46, rising to {D#,B}. That dyad, embedded in the trichord {D#,A,B}, is prolonged over mm. 47–48, where the trichord is embedded in the T11(APEX) that saturates the two measures. Then {D#,A,B} is prolonged yet farther over mm. 49–52, where it belongs to the prime form of DIM, the harmony that controls those measures. This prolongation of {D#,A,B} is portrayed by the closed slurs on example 4.25. Tentatively over mm. 51–52, and then definitively at m. 53, DIM moves down to T11(DIM). As that happens, the "overshoot" trichord {D#,A,B} moves down to {D,Ab,Bb}, which was the expected continuation from mm. 45–46. The {D,Bb} at the end of example 4.25 thus fills a chromatic gap as it marks the goal of the unidirectional line that began in m. 44. The dynamics over mm. 51–53 support that sense.

Example 4.25. A process going from the earlier melody (m. 44) to mm. 53–54.

Example 4.26 offers another transformational picture of mm. 49–52, emphasizing features other than those of example 4.22. The nodes on example 4.26 represent forms of DIM over mm. 49–52; the prime form of DIM is understood to be represented by the far left-hand node. The arrows of the example are labeled by numbers 1, 6, and so on, representing the transposition operations T1, T6, and so on. Thus, starting at the far left node, the 1-arrow indicates that DIM progresses to T1(DIM), as per the first arrow between the staves of example 4.22. On example 4.26, the 6-arrow from the left-hand node to the middle node indicates that DIM progresses to T6(DIM) as per the second arrow between the staves of example 4.22. On example 4.26, the 6-arrow from the middle node to the far-right node indicates that T6(DIM) moves on to DIM; this is where DIM goes up an octave in the music, at m. 51. The 11-arrow on example 4.26 indicates the high-register DIM moving down a semitone to T11(DIM), as portrayed in example 4.23.

In contrast to the dynamic and progressive structure of example 4.22, example 4.26 portrays a closed, symmetrical pattern. One notes in particular the sense of closure at m. 53, where the 11-move becomes definitive. This closure has already been discussed in other dimensions of the music.[20]

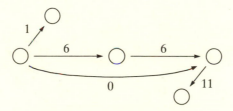

Example 4.26. An alternate transformational analysis of DIM-forms during mm. 49–52.

20. Example 4.26 and the graph of example 4.22 are both subgraphs of a larger graph. The larger graph could be obtained from example 4.26 by drawing 5-arrows on that example, one 5-arrow from the topmost node to the center node and another 5-arrow from the center node to the bottom node. The progressive diagonal chain of 5-arrows would disrupt the balanced symmetry of example 4.26. One could maintain

The left side of example 4.27 realizes the graph of example 4.26, using selected dyads from the DIM-forms of mm. 49–52. The dyads are specifically the 2-dyads that appear on the lower staff of the score over those measures, marking the ends of the sixteenth-triplet groups; these dyads are convenient tracers for the transformational picture. The temporal center of symmetry for the left side of example 4.27 is the bracketed figure {A3,B3}–{E♭,F4}–{A4,B4}. The {A,B} dyads are also the registral extremes for the passage, whereas the {E♭,F} dyad is the registral mean. The bracketed figure manifests the graph "T6 and T6 again is T0."

The bracketed material on the right side of example 4.27 transforms the left-side bracketed figure by T11. That expands the local T11 relation between the {A,B} and {A♭,B♭} dyads within m. 51. The right bracket of example 4.27 collects {A♭,B♭} dyads in three registers, bisecting them with {D,E} dyads in two registers. {D,E} also divides {A♭,B♭} temporarally: {A♭,B♭} dyads occur on the first beats of mm. 53 and 54, forte and *strident;* the dividing {D,E} is projected by pianissimo

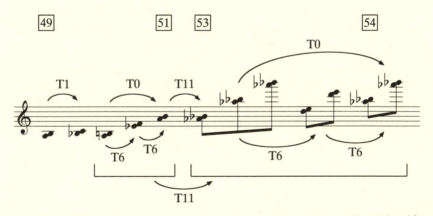

Example 4.27. Left side: a musical projection of example 4.26. Right side: the bracketed configuration to the left is transformed by T11 as the music continues.

---

that symmetry by drawing a 5-arrow from top to center node and a 7-arrow from bottom to center node. The result would, of course, violate the progressive spirit of example 4.22.

material within m. 53, a metrically weak pickup to the downbeat of m. 54. Those aspects of the music, together with the very audible T11-move from {A,B} to {A♭,B♭} during m. 51, support hearing the large-scale T11 arrow between the two bracketed sections of example 4.27.

The "6 + 6 = 0" graphs within examples 4.26 and 4.27 refer back to mm. 3–5, where the "sparking" D–A♭–D of the right hand divided the octave into tritones. Example 4.28 shows that the specific pitch-class gesture is recapitulated over mm. 52–56, except that D is now dividing A♭, rather than vice versa. D divides A♭ as discussed in connection with example 4.27 above. Example 4.28 also shows the persistence of D-dividing-A♭ in the harmony of mm. 57–58, where episode 2 begins.

The low D of m. 53 is a "low spark" or soft thud, rather like the low A♭ of m. 7. The D and the A♭, over mm. 3–6, were analyzed as the two centers of K-symmetry for the original black trichord {B♭,A♭,G♭}; the black trichord is subtly recalled by the {A♭,B♭} dyads of mm. 53–54. Those dyads recall the black trichord specifically by way of mm. 15–17, because of the registers involved.

In discussing the whole-tone pentachord of mm. 7–10, we noted that the new pitch class C disturbed the K-symmetry of {B♭,A♭,G♭} plus the bisectors {D,A♭}. C, we observed, generated some pressure for an arrival of E to complete both the whole-tone scale and the K-symmetry. The music of mm. 53–56 relaxes into just that whole-tone scale. This is the first time in the piece that a complete whole-tone scale has been projected in the harmony.[21]

Example 4.28. D bisects the octave A♭s (G♯s) into tritones, mm. 53–58.

21. A whole-tone scale governed aspects of long-range melodic structuring in

Because the whole-tone scale is so symmetrical and the music of mm. 55–56 is so regularly patterned, a number of partitionings are easily heard in that passage. For one thing, mm. 55–56 articulate into the black trichord {B♭,A♭,G♭} and the trichord we earlier called its "sister," {C,D,E}. The sister trichord figured prominently, one recalls, at the downbeat of m. 25. This trichordal partitioning of mm. 55–56 is projected by the division of the hands and by the pattern of the metrically strong sixteenths.

Example 4.28 suggests another partitioning for mm. 55–56. As shown in the example, the {D,A♭} dyad runs through every event of those measures. One can articulate the music into the {D,A♭} "line" of example 4.28 plus a concomitant contrapuntal "line" that runs against it. The contrapuntal line is isolated in example 4.29. As we shall see, the idea recurs.

The line of example 4.29 is grouped by brackets; the idea is to analyze the Cs as anacruses to the F♯s, and the Es as anacruses to the B♭s. That parallels the earlier remarks in which the Ds of these measures were analyzed as anacrustic to the A♭s. The notes of the sister trichord {C,D,E} are thus analyzed consistently as anacruses to the notes of the black trichord {F♯,A♭,B♭}. In that sense, the linear-contrapuntal partitioning is orthogonal ("perpendicular") to the trichordal partitioning.

Example 4.29. The contrapuntal line that runs along with example 4.28.

---

example 4.15 (stems up), but there was no foreground whole-tone scale in the harmony over that passage — only a whole-tone pentachord.

Episode 2 (mm. 57–64)

The top staff of example 4.30 sketches the melody of episode 2. One hears how this melody prolongs the whole-tone hexachord of mm. 53–56 through m. 62. The melodic C♯ of mm. 57–58 is the semitone-bisector for the signature dyad {C,D}; we have encountered C♯ in that capacity before.[22] On the top staff of example 4.30, the whole-tone set is completed by the B♭ of m. 61.

The melody of example 4.30 at m. 61, ending episode 2, is a variant of the melody from example 4.29, which ended episode 1. The melody expresses, inter alia, K-symmetry (about D, or about A♭): {C,F♯} and {E,B♭} are K-partners. The melody of m. 63, on example 4.30, also expresses K-symmetry: {E♭,A} and {G,C♯} are K-partners. In general, the 3-transpose of a K-symmetrical set will not be K-symmetrical. But that is the case here because the set in question, Forte-set 4–25, is doubly symmetrical. 4–25 comprises the forms of what we have called the "bisector" set BIS = {C,D,G♭,A♭}.

The melody of mm. 61–64 as a whole, on example 4.30, projects a complete octatonic set. This extends the intervallic implications of the "DIM" pentachord. Two forms of DIM are embedded in the first

Example 4.30. Principal melody, mm. 57–64; bass for mm. 59–64.

22. C♯ was so analyzed in connection with the melodic structure of the theme (example 4.14, m. 30).

hexachord of the total harmony in m. 61, a hexachord comprising the C- and F♯-major triads together. The hexachord is an octatonic subset. The same features obtain for the second hexachord of m. 61, which comprises E-major and B♭-major triads together. The same is also true for the second hexachord of m. 63, comprising G- and C♯-major triads together. The first hexachord of m. 63, comprising E♭-minor and A-major triads, is an octatonic subset; it does not, however, include any DIM-form as a subset.

The G♭ of the E♭-minor triad can be analyzed as a substitute for G♮ in an E♭-major triad, according to the norm for the remainder of mm. 61–64. The substitution makes the E♭-triad of m. 63 "very black," in contrast to the "very white" C-major triad of m. 61. In particular, the "black" E♭-minor triad goes with the black-note glissando of m. 63, just as the "white" C-major triad of m. 61 goes with the white-note glissando of that measure. The upward glissandos, pianissimo and *rubato*, make a striking effect following the downward loud black-note glissando at m. 17. The white and black glissandos, alternately drifting peacefully upwards during mm. 61–64, recur later at the acoustic climax of m. 87. There the white and black glissandos, loudly plummeting downwards, are violently superimposed rather than alternating.

The E♭ in m. 63 of example 4.30 is a bisector for the {C,F♯} of m. 61; the A in m. 63 is the other bisector for {C,F♯}. Furthermore, the C of m. 61 is a bisector for the {E♭,A} of m. 63, as is the F♯ of m. 61. Analogous relations obtain involving the {E,B♭} of m. 61 and the {G,C♯} of m. 63. G-bisecting-{E,B♭} is actually heard at the end of m. 62 (not shown on example 4.30). The idea of G-bisecting-{E,B♭} was already a feature of the APEX harmony in m. 25; the end of example 4.13 shows G in that capacity. C♯ was displayed at the end of example 4.17 as the other bisector of {E,B♭}-within-APEX.

So the bisections "6 = 3 + 3" and "6 = 9 + 9" were already suggested by the way the APEX harmony of the theme was approached and left. During mm. 61–64 of example 4.30, the tritone-bisection motif reaches full bloom, saturating the four-measure group: the notes of mm. 63–64 bisect the tritones of mm. 61–62; the notes of mm. 61–62 bisect the tritones of mm. 63–64. The bisections of "6 = 3 + 3 = 9 + 9" make a strong closure because of the complex symmetry just observed; that is related to the octatonic structuring. The closure is strong compositionally as well, for 6 is the last even interval to be bisected in the music. That is, we have already heard the bisections 4 = 2 + 2, 8 = 10 + 10, 2 = 1 + 1, 10 = 11 + 11, 2 = 7 + 7, 10 = 5 + 5, and 0 = 6 + 6. What we have not heard overtly, until mm. 61–64, is 6 = 3 + 3 and 6 = 9 + 9. Retroactively, and from m. 64 on, we shall hear the 3-cycles within DIM-form harmonies in this context.

Hearing mm. 63–64 on example 4.30 as "the bisectors of mm. 61–62," and hearing mm. 61–62 as "the bisectors of mm. 63–64," we shall be receptive to the idea that the black glissando and the white glissando mutually "bisect" each other. To some extent, we imagine the glissandos indefinitely extended in that capacity. To the extent that we do so, we are prepared for the mutual bisection of simultaneous white and black glissandos at the acoustic climax of m. 87.

The bass staff of example 4.30 elaborates the chromatic hexachord {B,C,C♯,D,D♯,E}. This level for the chromatic hexachord is associated with the music of mm. 20–24 plus the apex arrival on E at m. 25.

System a of example 4.31 shows how whole-tone harmonies govern mm. 57–60 as well as mm. 61–64 (in a different way). System b of the example reduces system a a stage further. On system a, the C♯s of mm. 57 and 58 are analyzed as appoggiaturas; the {B,C♯} of m. 59 is a double appoggiatura to B♯ and the {C♯,D♯} of m. 60 is a double appoggiatura to D♮. The stems-down line on the top staff of example 4.31a for mm. 59–60 thus repeats and intensifies the stems-down line on the top staff for mm. 57–58. When the appoggiaturas are reduced out on system b, the harmony of the four measures is heard moving through the whole-tone set of mm. 53–56, projecting first the BIS set {C,D,F♯,G♯} (mm. 57–58) and then forms of the whole-tone pentachord WTP (mm. 59–60).

The "harmony" of mm. 61–62 at this level is taken to be the BIS-form {C,F♯,E,B♭} outlined by the melody. The organum of the major triads makes a striking contrast in the foreground of the music, but

Example 4.31. Harmonic reduction of mm. 57–65.

the "middleground" {C,F♯,E,B♭} analyzed in example 4.31 connects very clearly with the rest of that example. Similar remarks obtain vis-à-vis the "harmony" of mm. 63–64 on example 4.31.

Example 4.31b shows how episode 2 is bounded by the J-symmetry of the set BIS, at m. 57, and by the K-symmetry of the BIS-forms at mm. 61–62 and mm. 63–64. The J-symmetry of BIS is emphasized all the more by the C♯s in the music of mm. 57–58. K-symmetry continues across the double bar of the example, into the T1(APEX) harmony that launches the first reprise at m. 65. The overall progression from J-symmetry (left side of example 4.31b) to K-symmetry (right side) is by now a familiar gesture in the piece. The voice-leading of example 4.31b, while following "the law of the nearest way," is also arranged so as to emphasize the arrival of T1(APEX) at m. 65 and especially the G♯ within that harmony. G♯ is a center of K-inversion. It receives special accentuation in the music because the incipit horn call of the theme leaps up to it.

146

First Reprise (mm. 65–70) and Episode 3 (mm. 71–78)

Example 4.32a shows the overall harmonic progression from the T1(APEX) that begins the first reprise (m. 65) to the APEX that begins the second reprise (m. 79). DIM-forms and whole-tone scale subsets mark intermediate stages in the large progression; semitone voice-leading is prominent within the passage as well. Those features recall the harmonic rhetoric that diminuted progressions between APEX-forms in the theme and variations section.[23]

Example 4.32. Progression from T1(APEX) at the first reprise to APEX at the second reprise.

23. Such rhetoric can be reviewed from example 4.18, mm. 31–39, and example 4.20, mm. 44–46.

The opening T1(APEX) of example 4.32 (m. 65) is inflected by the events of the cadenza (m. 67). In the analysis of example 4.32a, middle Db (m. 65–66) is neighbored by D♮ at m. 67, and the entire "Db^7 chord" within T1(APEX) is carried up in parallel T1-motion to the neighboring "D^7 chord" of m. 67, written with open noteheads. The Eb atop T1(APEX) at m. 65 remains, with open notehead, at m. 67; that gives rise to the "D^9 chord" with open noteheads at m. 67, a DIM-form that opens the cadenza. The cadenza is audibly octatonic; within it, one picks out, in particular, further DIM-forms {F,F♯,A,C,Eb} and {Ab,F♯,A,C,Eb}.[24] The neighboring events of the cadenza return to T1(APEX) at m. 68.

The middle section of the theme is changed so as to start from the incipit horn call; overall, the middle section then rises by only one semitone from the incipit. We shall have more to say about this feature of the first reprise. After the incipit motif is restated at mm. 68–69, the music up to m. 79 is based on middle-section thematic material, which rises quasi-sequentially, by a considerable number of semitones. This material is articulated in the music by textural changes at mm. 71 and 74; example 4.32a shows that these articulations coincide with stages in a prolongation of T1(APEX) as well. On the example, the asterisked harmonies at mm. 71 and 74 preserve the subset {F,Cb,Db,Eb} of T1(APEX).

Across m. 70 on example 4.32, a diagonal line connects the Ab of m. 70 to the Cb of m. 71; this represents a chromatic Zug between two notes of the T1(APEX) harmony. Meanwhile, the bass Db of m. 70 rises chromatically to E at m. 71, and E remains as a pedal tone over the subsequent measures. The chromatic line from Db to E is repeated an octave higher in m. 71/73 of the example. Events below E4, in the music of these measures, are represented an octave higher on example 4.32; the right-hand figuration in the music makes this representation plausible. In parallel sixths below the Db5-to-E5 line of m. 71/73 on the example, the chromatic line F4-to-G♯4 continues to rise chromatically from the Db4–E4 of mm. 70–71. At

24. One might consider holding the fortissimo D♮ of m. 65 through the cadenza, using the sostenuto pedal.

mm. 74–75 on the example, the notes with stems down show the line F–F♯–G–G♯ compacted into {F,G}–{G♭,A♭} and recapitulated in that form. In the music, this originally happens an octave higher, but there are ample grounds for asserting that the higher notes are representing events in register 4.[25]

In sum, as indicated by the stems-down notes over mm. 70–75 of example 4.32a, the chromatic rising action hereabouts is bounded by the tones D♭4 (m. 70) and A♭4 (mm. 74–76). Example 4.32b represents the chromatic gesture by a "middleground" beam connecting D♭4 and A♭4. One hears how the beamed gesture composes out the incipit horn call of the theme here, "in D♭." The end of the example indicates the foreground horn call "in C" for comparison. The example also indicates the E4 and F4 that articulate the beamed D♭–A♭ rise into D♭-to-E plus F-to-A♭. F-to-A♭ is a Zug within the T1(APEX) harmony; thus, F is graphed with an open notehead on the example. E, graphed with a filled-in notehead, is foreign to T1(APEX). The idea of rising-by-pc-interval-3 subsumes both F-to-A♭ and D♭-to-E; this idea seems to take its source from the octatonic- and DIM-form–saturated music of its recent past. Furthermore, the sense of a D♭ root is strong at the first reprise, and example 4.32b suggests some sense of E and F as alternate mediants for that root. The idea recurs strongly in a later event, at the downbeat of m. 96. There, just as the *Marseillaise* quote ends on its high sustained E, a D♭-major chord enters in a middle register, over the low tremolo on D♭1–A♭1. The low tremolo, projecting the ultimate "black" root of the piece, thus supports minor harmony as well as major harmony. In doing so, while supporting E, the "black" D♭ root undermines the "white"

25. We have just heard the D♭4–E4 line of mm. 70–71 represented by notes an octave higher during mm. 71–73. The spacing of the asterisked harmony at m. 74 of example 4.32 is "correct" for recalling the T1(APEX) spacing in m. 65 of the example. The asterisked harmony at m. 74 is T5(WTP), and the spacing is also "correct" for recalling the entire melody of variation 1 earlier (as isolated within example 4.14, mm. 35–38). The WTP harmony of mm. 74–75 becomes extremely mobile in register and spacing immediately thereafter, through m. 78; both spacings for WTP on example 4.32a are plausible. Measure 76 on the example gives the spacing that is manifest at m. 76 of the score.

tonality of the *Marseillaise*. The high E must be held until the effect registers — that is, until the quarter note E is sensed as a possible mediant (F♭) for the D♭–A♭ harmony, not only a mediant for the C harmony.

It was observed in note 25 that the set T5(WTP), as shown by example 4.32a at m. 74, recalls the melody of variation 1, which can be reviewed on example 4.14, mm. 35–38. T5(WTP) also recalls the harmony of the variation, which can be reviewed on example 4.18; there, as on example 4.32a, T5(WTP) was also an intermediate stage between T1(APEX) and APEX harmonies.

WTP, during mm. 74–78 of example 4.32a, is the original level of the whole-tone pentachord, from mm. 7–10. The partitioning of WTP on example 4.32a, as {G♭,A♭} + {B♭,C,D}, arises from the asserted voice-leading there and from the registral spacing of the harmony during mm. 76–78. In mm. 7–10, WTP arose as the union of the black trichord {B♭,A♭,G♭} with the signature dyad {C,D}. That partitioning of WTP is also manifest in the texturing of mm. 74–78, where it is projected by the right-hand and left-hand components of the score. In mm. 7–10 we observed that WTP built pressure toward an arrival of E, an arrival that occurred with the APEX event of m. 25, introducing the theme. Logically enough, the WTP harmony of mm. 74–78 leads directly into the APEX arrival of m. 79, where the second reprise of the theme commences at the original pitch-class level of m. 25. There is no big E downbeat at m. 79. The E downbeat, extending the {C,D} dyad to {C,D,E}, is withheld until the very end of the quote from the *Marseillaise,* at m. 96.

The change in the middle section of the melodic theme, at m. 67, has already been noted briefly. If the reprise were to have transposed the original theme literally, the pertinent pitches in m. 67 would have been D–B–A–C–B♭–E♭. Instead, the music gives D♭–B♭–A♭–B–A–D. This starts the middle section at the preceding incipit level; the effect is to strengthen the local D♭ root. In the original theme, the incipit C–G/C–A–G "passed through" D♭–B♭–A♭ to attain B–A–D; D♭ is thus heard as passing through the signature dyad {C,D}. In the first reprise, the incipit D♭–A♭/D♭–B♭–A♭ again continues into the middle section as Db–Bb–Ab, only then moving on to B–A–D and breaking off there. The emphasis now is on D as upper neighbor to Db. To the extent that we can continue hearing the piece "in Db," using for that purpose the big downbeat at m. 90 together with mm. 96–98, we will hear the Cs of the second reprise and of the *Marseillaise* as lower neighbors to Db. The focus changes from Db as bisector of the signature dyad to Db as center of events. (Both "tonal center" and "J-center," inter alia, are intended by the metaphor.)

Example 4.33a shows specifically how the figure of m. 67, with its Db–D gesture, is answered by the transposed figure at mm. 94–95, which projects the analagous C–Db gesture into the final Db cadence of the piece, centering the pitch class Db between D and C. The right-hand gesture of example 4.33a was prepared by the gesture of example 4.33b, heard during the second reprise. That gesture tries to continue on up to B–A–D, but then, at the *sff* quarter note Cb of m. 81, the music "remembers" the new form for the middle section of the reprised theme and subsides back down to Bb–Ab–Db.

Example 4.33. Melodic transformations, mm. 67–95, involving the "middle" element of the theme. Weight devolves onto Db.

Example 4.34 demonstrates another way in which the new form for the middle section of the theme contributes weight to the final D♭ root of the piece. Example 4.34a gives the middle section of the theme, at m. 67; it brackets the T1-relation between the first and the second of its unordered trichords. Example 4.34b shows the retrograde gesture; instead of moving up "from D♭ to D" it moves down "from D to D♭," emphasizing the return of the upper neighbor D to the "principal tone" D♭. The first trichord as a whole now moves down a semitone into the second trichord. Some individual downward semitones are beamed on the example: A moves down to A♭, B to B♭. The opening D of the example also moves down to the closing D♭.

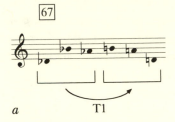

a   T1

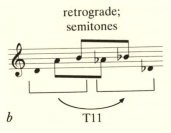

b   T11

c

Example 4.34. More melodic transformations, mm. 67ff.

Example 4.34c rearranges the ordering of example 4.34b so as to emphasize the beamed B–B♭ and A–A♭ T11-dyads between the opening D and the closing D♭. As indicated by the measure numbers above the example, this configuration is projected into the music of mm. 89–90. It is specifically the music that approaches and settles into "the big D♭ downbeat" at m. 90. The rearrangement of example 4.34b into example 4.34c emphasizes and liquidates the "semitone-down" idea.[26]

The discussion of examples 4.33 and 4.34 has brought the big D♭ downbeat of m. 90 and the D♭ cadence at m. 96 into connection with events of the first reprise. So did the discussion of example 4.32b, particularly with regard to the beamed D♭–A♭ Zug on that graph. At the opening of this essay there was little discussion of D♭ tonality or centricity in the coda; we simply assumed it was there. Now we have been directing analytic attention to ways in which the centric D♭ of the coda is established and supported. Measures 65ff. have been called a "first reprise" rather than a "false reprise." The reprise is "true" to the extent we hear the piece ending in D♭. To that extent, the second reprise is the "false" one. Or, rather, the term "false" is inappropriate for either of the reprises. There is no reason to underplay the C-major effect of the *Marseillaise* or of the C–G prolongation sketched in example 4.2, or of various other events in and around the music from the second reprise to the end. As noted earlier, "the piece contains not only the climactic C-major *Marseillaise* of example 4.2, and not only the D♭ structural downbeat of m. 90 as prepared by the climactic bomb of mm. 87ff., but also a crucial sort of metastable equilibrium between the two." The quote from the *Marseillaise* would lose all its poetic effect if the piece ended unequivocally "in C." And the final measures would lose their mood of unease, of concealed menace, if the piece ended unequivocally "in D♭." That would issue no challenge to the listener; if the battle is already lost, rather than subliminally threatening, there can be no call to arms.

---

26. The sort of semitone-partitioning manifest in example 4.34 bears a startling and interesting kinship to Schoenberg's mature hexachordal thought and practice. The String Trio, Op. 45, is particularly rich in similar hexachordal manipulations.

Second Reprise (m. 79) to the End

We have already noted how the accompaniment contour of m. 79, compared to that of m. 25, emphasizes the J-symmetry of the APEX set. The accompaniment of m. 79 also emphasizes how the trichord {B♭,C,D} is isolated in the lower register, a feature that clarifies and is clarified by the last few events sketched on example 4.32a. Measure 81 has just been discussed in connection with example 4.33. The rising chromatic motif of mm. 84–86 finds its goal at the *Marseillaise* citation; this was discussed in connection with example 4.2.

The chromatic rise during mm. 84–86 is texturally articulated into two 3-spans: T1 is applied three times to the opening trichord of m. 84; then T1 is applied three times to the opening gesture of m. 85. At pitch-class level, the opening melodic motif of m. 85 repeats the final melodic trichord of m. 84; hence the bass line of mm. 84–86 moves by C–E♭ plus E♭–F♯, filling a "3 + 3 = 6" graph. Each other "part" of the trichordal motif fills the same graph.

The "diminished" character of the graph moves into the foreground harmony of mm. 85–86, where DIM-forms are heard on the offbeats, as on example 4.35. The spacing of the DIM-forms there is meant to recall the spacing of the mobile DIM-forms on example 4.22, whose music (mm. 49–52) has the same melodic rhythm and contour. The total rhythm of m. 52 includes the same syncopations as those of mm. 85–86.

The chromatic rise of mm. 84–86 is like the chromatic rise of mm. 70–74 on example 4.32 in that both articulate a pair of 3-spans. On

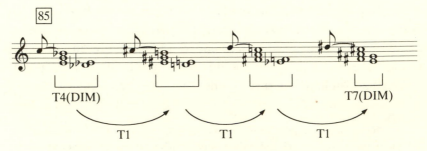

Example 4.35. Transformations of DIM-forms, mm. 85–86.

example 4.32 the 3-spans are adjacent, as summarized by the D♭–E and F–A♭ of example 4.32b. The overall rise then projects the "horn call" D♭–A♭. Over mm. 84–86 the two 3-spans overlap, as C–E♭ plus E♭–F♯ in the bass, to project an overall tritone rise. As example 4.2 shows, the G that will complete the overall rise, projecting a middle-ground horn call C–G, is the G that begins the *Marseillaise* quote.

About the climactic bomb, its aftermath, and the coda, much has already been said. Example 4.36 collates a number of further observations that qualify the effect of the cadence at m. 96. Example 4.36a shows how the *Marseillaise* quote, plus the C-major incipit motif from the theme, projects the pentatonic set T7(PENT). The "T7" is generated by the 7-relation in m. 7 between the signature dyad {C,D} and the upper 2–2 dyad {G,A} of the white trichord. In mm. 92–96 the T7-relation between the same dyads is audible in the temporal relation of the {C,D}s within the *Marseillaise* to the immediately following {G,A} dyads within the reminiscences of the theme. The dyads are bracketed on example 4.36a. The registral interval of pitch transposition is −5, which is 7 as a pitch-class interval. We earlier observed that T7(PENT) was already latent in the music of mm. 25–29, arising from the E–D–C of the APEX figuration, plus the C–G/C–A–G of the theme. In example 4.36a we hear the C–G/C–A–G of the theme, and we are also made aware of the trichord C–D–E, particularly as the *Marseillaise* approaches m. 96.

An echo of the APEX harmony itself is also present at just that moment. Example 4.36b focuses on the relevant notes, which bring to our attention the embedding of the entire *Marseillaise* quotation within the pitch classes of APEX. Indeed, APEX consists precisely of the pitch classes to be found within "Aux armes, citoyens! Formez vos batallions! Marchons, marchons . . . " together with the pitch class B♭. The B♭ makes APEX J-symmetrical. Example 4.13 is interesting to review in this connection, fanning out as it does from the J-symmetrical signature dyad.[27]

Example 4.36c shows a reminiscence that is tricky to catch at first,

27. These matters may have something to do with the one-flat signature for the piece. I find it difficult to hear the piece "in F," or even in "Mixolydian C."

Example 4.36. Reminiscences gather around the downbeat of m. 96.

by ear or in performance. A small nucleus of registrally and temporally contiguous material projects the entire ordered white trichord F–G–A in retrograde and the beginning of the ordered black trichord B♭–A♭–G♭. In connection with example 4.4, the point was made that the trichords could be heard as transposed retrogrades of each other. Example 4.36c shows the ordered white trichord retrograding itself to bring out this relation. As befits the cadential situation, the trichord now descends to F at m. 96, rather than rising from F.[28]

In order to catch example 4.36c in performance, one can pay particular attention to the staccato marks on the A–G and the legato mark on the F, thereby projecting A–G as anacrusis to F. Different hands will find different expedients. Various fingerings on A–G are useful for experimentation: 3–2, or 2–1, or even 3–1. 3–2 on A–G may enable one to play F with the thumb of the right hand, an interesting option even though it runs counter to the composer's notation. It automatically groups the trichord A–G–F, detaching the contrapuntally active F from the harmonic A♭ and D♭ that lie immediately beneath it.

Example 4.36d shows a momentary DIM-form straddling the barline of mm. 95–96 that also contributes color to the cadence. The G, B♭, and E in the right hand are part of the APEX reminiscence; the three tones are J-symmetrical, as is APEX, and the pedal D♭ is a center of J-symmetry. The end of example 4.17 shows an earlier instance of D♭ (C♯) serving in this capacity over mm. 33–34. Indeed, that gave rise to the first DIM-form harmony in the piece, shown at the beginning of example 4.18.

Just as the low pedal D♭ is a center of symmetry for the J-symmetrical APEX of example 4.36b, so is the low pedal A♭ a center of symmetry for the K-symmetrical T7(PENT) of example 4.36a. We pointed this out earlier, in connection with the other centers for J and K, G and D, respectively, in the *Marseillaise* quote at the downbeats of mm. 92 and 93 respectively.

The *Marseillaise* quote is thus involved in a supersaturated texture of reminiscences that congregate about the downbeat of m. 96. The quotation implicates the signature dyad {C,D} in example 4.36a, particularly in the approach to m. 93. The {C,D} dyad extends to the ordered trichord C–D–E approaching m. 96, and that implicates in

28. A G♭ at the end of example 4.36c would be otiose. It would make the reminiscence glaringly audible, rather than subtly suggestive. The semitone relation between F and G♭ would be dubious as well. It would distract attention from the semitone relations between F and the high E of the *Marseillaise,* as mediants of D♭ major and C major, respectively, and as a double mediant F/F♭ for the D♭ major/minor root.

example 4.36b the high E downbeat of m. 25 as well as the E–D–C trichord that begins that measure. Example 4.36d implicates the high E downbeat of the quotation with the high E downbeat of m. 25 as well, via mm. 33–34. Example 4.36c at first seems not to involve the *Marseillaise* quotation, but in fact it does. If the quotation were to continue ("qu'un sang impur . . . ") it would go beyond the high E of m. 96, exactly to the trichord F–G–A. But, says example 4.36c, we are through with F–G–A now; the music is cadencing so as to retrograde the gesture into A–G–F.[29]

It would be inexact to think of the *Marseillaise* as a cantus firmus or paraphrase source here. The conception, I think, is more like this: In the fireworks proper we have just witnessed a brilliant display of design, color, transformation, and organized motif. We might imagine ourselves standing somewhere around the Trocadéro or the Eiffel Tower, surrounded by other brilliant symbols of modern French design and civilization. Suddenly we are reminded, by music from somewhere else, far away, out of tune, that the display is meant to celebrate some "old" and "remote" ideas of a republic based upon liberty, equality, and fraternity. We can imagine the sound of the band reaching us from the old, remote Place de la Bastille.[30] But do we notice that reminder? We sense vaguely (especially at m. 96) that there are sensible connections between the old music and the display

29. Can one meaningfully assert "qu'un sang impur," including the final low D of that phrase, in the music at the beginning of m. 7? The low D there is embedded in the first signature-dyad of the piece, whose indication *marqué* has been noted and discussed; *Debussy nous marque quelque chose* here. It is difficult for me to imagine how one might make such an analytic assertion seem methodologically significant, or even plausible. Yet the idea seems attractive enough to mention. To make the idea work analytically, one would either have to locate a hidden quotation of "abreuve nos sillons" somewhere in the music — I have not — or give a good rationale for the absence of such a quotation. It is much safer to deny significance to the suggested quotation at m. 7 so that the quoted material ends with the call to arms, at the high E of m. 96. Then example 4.36c can be read as engaging what does *not* continue to happen in the quotation, rather than throwing us cyclically back to some asserted continuation in m. 7.

30. The conceit will work for 1913 at least. Now that the official operatic establishment has become installed in the Place de la Bastille, the idea no longer works so well. (But that is my point, isn't it?)

we have just witnessed. But no sooner do we sense that than the old music vanishes and we are suspended, for the last three measures, in the here-and-now of the nocturnal, vaguely "dräuenden" D♭.

I cannot share the militant nationalism of Debussy's personal thoughts. But I find the rest of the conception suggested above remarkable, no less so for the ostensible naturalism with which the composition conceals the emotional depth of the idea. Despite the many spasms of American militant nationalism over the past half-century, I am still patriot enough to be bothered that at the climax of our July Fourth celebrations we perform Tchaikovsky's *1812 Overture*, celebrating not our Declaration of Independence, nor our Constitution, but rather the victory of a Russian Czar over a Napoleonic army.

REFERENCES

Baker, James. 1986. *The Music of Alexander Scriabin.* New Haven: Yale University Press.

Bamberger, Jeanne. 1986. Cognitive Issues in the Development of Musically Gifted Children. Chap. 17 in *Conceptions of Giftedness,* ed. Robert J. Sternberg and Janet E. Davidson. 388–413. New York: Cambridge University Press.

Cherlin, Michael. 1983. The Formal and Dramatic Organization of Schoenberg's Moses und Aron. Ph.D. diss., Yale University.

Clough, John. 1989. David Lewin, *Generalized Musical Intervals and Transformations. Music Theory Spectrum* 11 no. 2 (Fall):226–31.

Cone, Edward T. 1962. Stravinsky: The Progress of a Method. *Perspectives of New Music* 1/1 (Fall 1962):18–26.

Cook, Nicholas. 1987. *A Guide to Musical Analysis.* New York: George Braziller.

Cooper, Grosvenor W., and Leonard B. Meyer. 1960. *The Rhythmic Structure of Music.* Chicago: University of Chicago Press.

Forte, Allen. 1973. *The Structure of Atonal Music.* New Haven: Yale University Press.

———. 1988a. New Approaches to the Linear Analysis of Music. *Journal of the American Musicological Association* 41:315–48.

———. 1988b. Pitch-Class Set Genera and the Origin of Modern Harmonic Species. *Journal of Music Theory* 32:187–270.

———. 1991. Debussy and the Octatonic. *Music Analysis* 10:125–69.

Harvey, Jonathan. 1975. The Music of Stockhausen. Berkeley: University of California Press.

Hyer, Brian. 1989. Tonal Intuitions in *Tristan und Isolde.* Ph.D. diss., Yale University.

Lesure, François, and Roger Nichols, eds. 1987. *Debussy Letters.* Trans. Roger Nichols. Cambridge, Mass.: Harvard University Press.

Lewin, David. 1967. A Study of Hexachord Levels in Schoenberg's Violin Fantasy. *Perspectives of New Music* 6/1 (Fall–Winter 1967):18–32.

———. 1986. Music Theory, Phenomenology, and Modes of Perception." *Music Perception* 3:327–92.

———. 1987. *Generalized Musical Intervals and Transformations.* New Haven: Yale University Press.

———. 1991. Some Problems and Resources of Music Theory. *Journal of Music Theory Pedagogy* 5/2:111–32.

Lockspeiser, Edward. 1972. *Debussy.* New York: McGraw-Hill.

Lorenz, Alfred. 1926. *Das Geheimnis der Form bei Richard Wagner.* Vol. 2. Berlin: Max Hesse.

Narmour, Eugene. 1977. *Beyond Schenkerism.* Chicago: The University of Chicago Press.

Parks, Richard S. 1989. *The Music of Claude Debussy.* New Haven: Yale University Press.

Rahn, Jay. 1985. *A Theory for All Music.* Toronto: University of Toronto Press.

Straus, Joseph. 1987. The Problem of Prolongation in Post-Tonal Music. *Journal of Music Theory* 31:1–21.

INDEX